"How to..." Sermon Outlines

Russell E. Spray

BAKER BOOK HOUSE
Grand Rapids, Michigan 49506

ISBN: 0-8010-8252-8

Fourth printing, October 1989

Formerly published under the titles:
*How To . . . Sermon Outlines 1, How To . . . Sermon Outlines 2, How
To . . . Sermon Outlines 3.*

Printed in the United States of America

Contents

Introduction

These *"How To . . ." Sermon Outlines* may be used by all who speak on spiritual themes—ministers, teachers, and Christian laymen and women.

It is the prayer of author and publisher that these outlines will bring sparkle and enrichment to the speaking ministry of those who use them and that God may be glorified.

—*Russell E. Spray*

1. How to A-S-K in Prayer

"Ask, and it shall be given you; seek, and ye shall find; knock, and it shall be opened unto you" (Matt. 7:7).

I. A-sk with Simplicity
"Ask, and it shall be given you" (Matt. 7:7).
- A. Asking gets the response of a gift. Children receive gifts from their parents because they ask.
- B. We are God's children. He wants us to ask in childlike faith. We are to ask largely (Matt. 7:11).
- C. We are to keep on asking. Some do not ask at all. Many more do not continue to ask (Matt. 7:8).

II. S-eek with Intensity
"Seek, and ye shall find" (Matt. 7:7).
- A. Seeking brings discovery. We discover God's Word, His promises, and His blessings (Jer. 29:13).
- B. Search for the deeper, richer values to be found in Christ. Treasures are discovered in the secret place of the Most High (Ps. 91:1).
- C. Precious souls—far more valuable than silver and gold— are found when we seek out the lost and win them to Christ (Dan. 12:3).

III. K-nock with Persistency
"Knock, and it shall be opened unto you" (Matt. 7:7).
- A. Persistent knocking gets a response.
- B. Persistent knocking means prevailing prayer, fasting, all night in prayer, perhaps.
- C. Persistent prayer gains an entrance into the secret treasures of divine resources (Isa. 45:1-3).
- D. Persistent knocking calls for determination. It takes time for God to grow an oak or a rose. It takes time for Him to answer certain of our prayers (Matt. 7:8).

2. How to Avoid Being L-O-S-T

"For the Son of man is come to save that which was lost" (Matt. 18:11).

I. L-ost Love
"Thou hast left thy first love" (Rev. 2:4).

A. In marriage—it is sad to hear the words, "I don't love him [or her] anymore." Where children are involved, it is still more difficult.

B. Churches sometimes lose their love. The members find fault, criticize, and complain. This always spells defeat if love is not restored.

C. The remedy for lost love is repentance, faith, and, perhaps, restitution (Rev. 2:5).

II. Lost O-pportunities
"Whosoever shall save his life shall lose it" (Mark 8:35).

A. Almost everyone has lost opportunities pertaining to finances, jobs, and health.

B. Many have lost opportunities to help others, to witness, to win souls to Christ.

C. Some opportunities are lost forever. Some may be recaptured. New opportunities must be seized and utilized.

III. Lost S-oul
"What shall a man give in exchange for his soul?" (Mark 8:37).

A. Loss of finances can be sad. Loss of health, even worse. To lose one's soul is the most devastating loss of all.

B. There are two conditions of the soul that determines its destiny—to be saved or to be lost.

C. The power of choice is ours. Through God's love all may be saved (John 3:16).

IV. Lost T-ime
"The harvest is past, the summer is ended, and we are not saved" (Jer. 8:20).

A. As long as time remains, love can be recaptured, opportunities retrieved, fortunes regained, health restored.

B. When time has run out, it is too late for the soul that is lost. How much time is left for you?

C. We are only sure of the now. *Now* is the accepted time. *Now* is the day of salvation (2 Cor. 6:2).

3. How to Avoid Excuse-making

Scripture Reading: Luke 14:16-27

"And they with one consent began to make excuse" (Luke 14:18).

I. Excuse of Property
"The first said . . . I have bought a piece of ground, I must needs go and see it: I pray thee have me excused" (Luke 14:18).
- A. We live in a materialistic age. The love of possessions has captured the hearts of millions.
- B. We must keep our possessions in the right perspective.
- C. We should not use possessions as an excuse for being less than our best for God (Matt. 6:33).

II. Excuse of Pursuit
"And another said, "I have bought five yoke of oxen, and I go to prove them: I pray thee have me excused" (Luke 14:19).
- A. These are busy times. We have more time-saving gadgets than ever before but still we have less time.
- B. Christians should not be overtaken with the hurry, scurry of these busy days.
- C. We must make time for God and give Him first place in our lives.

III. Excuse of Person
"And another said, "I have married a wife, and therefore I cannot come" (Luke 14:20).
- A. Blaming other people is perhaps the most often used excuse. We tend to blame others for our failures, disappointments, troubles, and so forth.
- B. Other people may also be blamed for one's lack of service to God or for not accepting Christ as Savior.
- C. Christians must keep their eyes centered on Jesus Christ, who is the author and finisher of their faith (Heb. 12:2).

4. How to Be a Good Samaritan

Scripture Reading: Luke 10:25-37

I. The Seeking of Love
"But a certain Samaritan, as he journeyed, came where he was" (Luke 10:33).
A. The priest and Levite passed by on the other side.
B. Christ came to earth—where we are—to seek and save.
C. If we are to win souls, we must go where the lost are, seeking them out.

II. The Sympathy of Love
"He had compassion on him" (Luke 10:33).
A. The Good Samaritan had compassion on the poor man who had fallen among thieves.
B. Christ has great compassion for all mankind.
C. If we are to help others, we must have a heart of love and be filled with compassion.

III. The Service of Love
"And bound up his wounds, pouring in oil and wine" (Luke 10:34).
A. The Good Samaritan did not stop with seeking and feeling compassion, but he *did* something for the man he found and felt for.
B. Christ always helps those who seek after Him.
C. Do we ofttimes see the needs and feel compassion for others but fail to do anything to help them?

IV. The Selflessness of Love
"And set him on his own beast, and brought him to an inn, and took care of him" (Luke 10:34).
A. The Good Samaritan denied himself to help this man.
B. Christ denied Himself, giving His life for the world.
C. We should deny ourselves by becoming involved in caring for the needs of others.

V. The Spending of Love

"And whatsoever thou spendest more . . . I will repay thee"
(Luke 10:35).

A. The Good Samaritan paid a price to help someone else.

B. It cost Jesus His life's blood to save us.

C. It will cost us time, talent, and treasure to help those in need and to win the lost to Christ.

5. How to Be Effective for God

"If any man will come after me, let him deny himself . . . and follow me" (Matt. 16:24).

I. Prevailing Prayer
"Effectual fervent prayer . . . availeth much" (James 5:16).
A. Prayers of petition—for our own needs and the needs of others—are effective when accompanied by faith.
B. Prayers of praise are effective and bring the immediate approval of God.

II. Powerful Word
"For the word of God is quick, and powerful" (Heb. 4:12).
A. God's Word to mankind is a chart, a map, showing us the "how" to successful living.
B. God's inspired Word points the way to salvation and eternal life. Its use makes effective soul-winners.

III. Positive Faith
"Jesus . . . said, Daughter . . . thy faith hath made thee whole" (Matt. 9:22).
A. This afflicted woman came to Jesus, determined to touch only the hem of His garment. Her faith was emphatic, certain that she would be healed.
B. All things are possible with positive faith. This kind of faith makes us effective for God.

IV. Persevering Love
"For the love of Christ constraineth us" (2 Cor. 5:14).
A. There is no defense against a love that doesn't quit or give up. It breaks down walls of resentments, hurts, and misunderstandings.
B. Persevering love includes compassion and empathy. It enables us to be effective as we relate to others by endeavoring to put ourselves in their place.

V. Persistent Effort
"Ye are my witnesses, saith the Lord" (Isa. 43:10).
A. We are to witness to others about the saving power of Jesus Christ.
B. To be effective we must be persistent and patient in our efforts. We must never give up. The value of a soul is beyond estimation.

6. How to Become As Little Children

Scripture Reading: Matthew 18:1-6

"Except ye be converted, and become as little children, ye shall not enter into the kingdom of heaven" (Matt. 18:3).

I. Practice Humility
"Whosoever therefore shall humble himself as this little child . . ." (Matt. 18:4).
A. Little children realize they are small and must look up to grown-ups. They are aware of their lack of strength and wisdom. They ask for help and guidance.
B. God wants us to be aware of our lack of strength and of our inability to understand everything. He wants us to ask Him for assistance and wisdom (James 1:5).

II. Practice Trust
"Trust in the Lord with all thine heart" (Prov. 3:5).
A. Trust is a wonderful characteristic of little children. They trust their parents implicitly to meet their needs.
B. Many people are trusting in materialistic pursuits and depending on their own abilities.
C. God wants His children to trust Him completely to meet their needs (Phil. 4:19).

III. Practice Light-heartedness
"Casting all your care upon him; for he careth for you" (1 Peter 5:7).
A. It is normal for little children to be light-hearted and carefree. There are exceptions, such as those coming from broken homes, etc.
B. God wants His children to be light-hearted and carefree, too. He is able to bear their burdens (1 Peter 5:7).

IV. Practice Persistence
"Let us hold fast the profession of our faith" (Heb. 10:23).
A. A little child falls many times but he never gives up until he learns to walk.
B. Christians make blunders and mistakes, but they should keep trying and refuse to give up.

V. Practice Anticipation

"I press toward the mark for the prize . . ." (Phil. 3:14).

A. Children continually look ahead with anticipation.

B. Discouragement is short-lived with children. They look to the future with hope.

C. Christians should look ahead with anticipation, too. They should look for and expect the best to come (John 14:1-3).

7. How to Bring Meaning to L-I-F-E

"I am crucified with Christ: nevertheless I live; yet not I, but Christ liveth in me" (Gal. 2:20).

I. L-ove Brings Meaning

"If we love one another, God dwelleth in us . . ." (1 John 4:12).

A. Love is necessary for life to have meaning. To love and be loved is a built-in psychological need.

B. The more love we give, the greater capacity we have to receive.

C. God's love brings meaning—it reaches through us to others with compassion, understanding, and a helping hand (1 John 3:14).

II. I-nvolvement Brings Meaning

"He that abideth in me, and I in him . . . bringeth forth much fruit" (John 15:5).

A. Involvement in one's work, hobbies, exercise is helpful. Involvement in charity and hospital work is also good.

B. Life becomes more meaningful when we are involved in God's work—church activities, intercessory prayer, and sharing Christ with others.

C. Involvement precedes the harvest (1 John 3:18).

III. F-aith Brings Meaning

"This is the victory . . . even our faith" (1 John 5:4).

A. The Christian life is a life of faith, for we are to use the shield of faith to defeat Satan at every onslaught.

B. Everything good and right is possible through faith.

C. Faith pleases God and brings meaning to life (Heb. 11:6).

IV. E-ternal Values Bring Meaning

"Lay not up . . . treasures upon earth . . . but lay up treasures in heaven" (Matt. 6:19-20).

A. Those who live only for selfish and temporal pursuits are most unhappy.

B. Life can have meaning only when eternal values are kept in proper focus.

C. Eternal values include liberal giving of our time, talents, and treasures and the hope of eternal life (1 John 5:13).

8. How to Defeat Satan

"Submit yourselves therefore to God. Resist the devil, and he will flee from you" (James 4:7).

I. **Think the Right Thoughts (This involves the mind.)**
   "Think on these things" (Phil. 4:8).
   A. Think positively, dwelling on things of good report.
   B. Expect the best. Faith brings victory over Satan (1 John 5:4).

II. **See the Right Sights (This involves the eyes.)**
   "Looking unto Jesus . . ." (Heb. 12:2).
   A. Many see only the faults of others.
   B. We defeat Satan by looking for the good in others and keeping our eyes on Jesus.

III. **Hear the Right Sounds (This involves the ears.)**
   "Faith cometh by hearing . . ." (Rom. 10:17).
   A. We hear many sounds—music, traffic, conversations, TV . . .
   B. We should listen for the voice of God, striving to hear His softest whispers.

IV. **Say the Right Words (This involves the voice.)**
   "For out of the abundance of the heart the mouth speaketh" (Matt. 12:34).
   A. Many speak resentful, unkind, and critical words.
   B. Christians should speak words of love and understanding, sharing Christ whenever opportunity affords.

V. **Do the Right Things (This involves the hands.)**
   "In every good work to do His will . . ." (Heb. 13:21).
   A. Defeat Satan by meaningful action.
   B. Do good to others, fulfilling God's will (Matt. 5:16).

VI. **Go to the Right Places (This involves the feet.)**
   "I was glad when they said unto me, Let us go into the house of the Lord" (Ps. 122:1).
   A. Many are on the move, following after selfish pursuits and pleasures.
   B. Christians should go for God. Go to church. Lend a helping hand. Witness for Christ. Win the lost to Him.

VII. Belong to the Right Person (This involves the heart.)

"I have chosen you" (John 15:16).

A. Defeat Satan by giving God first place in your affections.
B. With His Spirit abiding in our hearts we are more than conquerors. Satan is a defeated foe (1 John 4:4).

9. How to Define God's Blessings

Scripture Reading: Psalm 121

"My help cometh from the Lord, which made heaven and earth" (Ps. 121:2).

I. Providential Help
"I will lift up mine eyes unto the hills, from whence cometh my help. My help cometh from the Lord . . ." (Ps. 121:1-2).
A. Great strides have been made in helping mankind find a better life. Medical and scientific discoveries have benefited many.
B. God's help is a far greater blessing. He can forgive sins. He can lift burdens and give peace. He can comfort in times of bereavement.

II. Personal Attention
"He will not suffer thy foot to be moved: he that keepeth thee . . . shall neither slumber nor sleep" (Ps. 121:3-4).
A. In today's busy, overpopulated world it is difficult to get personalized attention.
B. God's blessings include His personal attention. He keeps watch over each of us day and night, for He never slumbers nor sleeps.

III. Protective Care
"The Lord is thy keeper . . . The sun shall not smite thee by day, nor the moon by night" (Ps. 121:5-6).
A. Our modern world is a place of danger and risk. The streets are unsafe by both night and day.
B. God blesses His children with protecting care—protection from harm, strength for the day, grace for the trials.

IV. Preserving Power
"The Lord shall preserve thee from all evil . . . even forevermore" (Ps. 121:7-8).
A. Preserve—"To keep from injury or destruction; defend from evil; save" (Webster).
B. Earth's treasures are temporal and do not last.
C. God's preserving power never fails (2 Tim. 1:12).

10. How to Describe a Christian

"Yet if any man suffer as a Christian, let him not be ashamed; but let him glorify God on this behalf" (1 Peter 4:16).

I. In Christ

"Therefore if any man be in Christ, he is a new creature" (2 Cor. 5:17).

A. The Christian is *in* Christ, his sins are forgiven, and his guilt is gone. He is a new creature.

B. Christ is *in* the surrendered Christian, cleansing and filling him with His divine love. He is there to lead, guide, and direct. He will give him power for service.

II. Like Christ

"Leaving us an example, that ye should follow his steps" (1 Peter 2:21).

A. The desire of the Christian should be to act as Christ would act, to do the things that He would do and speak the words He would speak.

B. We may be *like* Christ by reading the Bible daily, praying often, and being kind and compassionate to other people.

III. For Christ

"Glorify God in your body, and in your spirit . . ." (1 Cor. 6:20).

A. The Christian is *for* Christ as a good soldier is for his country. He is willing to endure afflictions and persecution for Christ.

B. The Christian should be ready to share Christ with others and to give his time, talents, and treasures for Him.

IV. With Christ

"And so shall we ever be with the Lord" (1 Thess. 4:17).

A. Here and now, the Lord is *with* the Christian. He has promised never to leave nor forsake His own.

B. Hereafter, *with* Christ, there will be no burdens, no trials, no suffering. The Christian shall be forever with the Lord.

11. How to Describe God's People

"But ye are a chosen generation, a royal priesthood, an holy nation, a peculiar people; that ye should shew forth the praises of him who hath called you out of darkness into his marvelous light" (1 Peter 2:9).

I. A Chosen People
"But ye are a chosen generation . . ." (1 Peter 2:9).
A. Chosen—"Selected from a number; picked out; choice; elect" (Webster).
B. We are not chosen because of race, creed, talent, money, or our works (Titus 3:5).
C. We are chosen because God loves and had mercy on us (John 3:16).

II. A Royal People
"Ye are a . . . royal priesthood . . ." (1 Peter 2:9).
A. Royal—"Characteristic of or befitting a king; magnificent; kingly; majestic" (Webster).
B. God's people are royal because of their adoption into the family of God (Rom. 8:14-15).
C. God's people are royal because of their relationship to the triune God (Rom. 8:16-17).

III. A Holy People
"Ye are a . . . holy nation . . ." (1 Peter 2:9).
A. Holy—"Set apart to the worship of God; spiritually whole—unimpaired innocence or proved virtue; godly" (Webster).
B. We should willingly set ourselves apart to the worship of God by giving ourselves to Him in surrender and consecration. (Rom. 12:1).
C. The Holy Spirit cleanses the heart of the surrendered Christian and gives him power for service.

IV. A Peculiar People
"Ye are a . . . peculiar people" (1 Peter 2:9).
A. Peculiar—"Belonging to an individual; privately owned; not common—private property" (Webster).

B. The Christian who completely belongs to God is not his own. This sets him apart and makes him different from the world.

C. We should glorify God by giving Him first place in our lives.

s to number our days, that we may apply our hearts unto wisaom" (Ps. 90:12).

I. Spiritual Subtraction
"He was manifested to take away our sins" (1 John 3:5).

A. Small children know that two-take-away-two leaves zero.

B. The principle of Christ's forgiveness should be learned early in life. Christ "takes away" the sins of those who repent and believe on Him (1 John 2:1).

II. Spiritual Division
"He shall divide the spoil with the strong . . . he bare the sin of many . . ." (Isa. 53:12).

A. Christ gave Himself for us, dividing a portion with the great. He is our example (1 John 2:6).

B. We should divide our time, talent, testimony, and treasure, paying the tithe, or tenth, of our income so the church can meet its obligations and do the work God has given us to do (Mal. 3:10).

III. Spiritual Addition
"And beside this, giving all diligence, add . . ." (2 Peter. 1:5).

A. We are to grow in the grace of Jesus Christ by adding, or increasing in, the fruits and virtues of the Spirit (2 Peter. 1:5-7).

B. Begin with faith and end with love. Adding these many fruits of the Spirit to life will settle, establish, and strengthen the Christian.

IV. Spiritual Multiplication
"The number of the disciples was multiplied . . ." (Acts 6:1).

A. Some have difficulty with the multiplication tables.

B. It is fascinating to observe the great increase multiplication brings.

C. God wants the number of His disciples to be increased. This is done through the winning of others to Him. As we do this we receive multiplied blessings (Jude 2).

13. How to Evaluate Faith

Scripture Reading: Ephesians 6:10-18

"Above all, taking the shield of faith, wherewith ye shall be able to quench all the fiery darts of the wicked" (Eph. 6:16).

I. Its Importance
"Above all . . ." (Eph. 6:16).
A. Faith is important because it is the way to receive God. He comes not by feelings or sight but by faith.
B. Faith is important because it is the way to receive from God. God provides for us according to our faith.
C. Faith is important because it can be a way of life. The just are to live by faith (Rom. 1:17).

II. Its Availability
"Taking the shield of faith . . ." (Eph. 6:16).
A. Faith is available because it is God's will that we have it.
B. We cannot buy faith; we cannot earn it; we are to simply take it. It is God's free gift.
C. Faith increases with practice and use. Faith works as we work our faith.

III. Its Power
"Wherewith ye shall be able . . ." (Eph. 6:16).
A. There is great power in faith—the power of God. The Bible says that nothing is impossible to those who believe.
B. The power of faith enables us, with the apostle Paul, to do all things through Christ's strength.
C. The power of faith enables us to live victoriously, to serve effectively, and to praise the Lord whole-heartedly.

IV. Its Extent
"To quench all the fiery darts of the wicked" (Eph. 6:16).
A. There is no problem too big for faith, no mountain too high, no valley too deep, no burden too heavy, no task too difficult.
B. By faith we are able to quench, extinguish, put out *all* the fiery, flaming darts of the wicked one.
C. Its extent is great because faith joins the Christian to Omnipotence.

14. How to Explain the G-O-S-P-E-L

"For I am not ashamed of the gospel of Christ; for it is the power of God unto salvation to every one that believeth" (Rom. 1:16).

I. G-ood News
"Behold, I bring you good tidings of great joy . . ." (Luke 2:10).
- A. Gospel means *good news:* Christ's coming fulfilled the prophecies made hundreds of years before by Micah, Isaiah, and others.
- B. The *good news* of the Gospel is that Christ came to be the Savior of the world.

II. O-pportunity
"And the gospel must first be published among all nations" (Mark 13:10).
- A. In this world of greed opportunities are not equal for all. Social injustice, disease, and poverty abounds.
- B. The Gospel means opportunity for all. Christ is the answer for the sin problem, social injustice, etc. He is no respecter of persons.

III. S-alvation
"For it is the power of God unto salvation . . ." (Rom. 1:16).
- A. Sin is the real problem. Wars, strifes, and so on are products of sin.
- B. The Gospel means salvation from sin. Christ came to destroy Satan's works and set men free from sin's bondage.

IV. P-eace
"Preach the gospel of peace . . ." (Rom. 10:15).
- A. Despite its scientific, educational, and cultural achievements, there is still need for peace on earth.
- B. The gospel of Jesus brings needed peace, lasting peace.

V. E-verlasting
"Having the everlasting gospel to preach unto them . . ." (Rev. 14:6).
- A. Houses, land, silver, gold, beauty, and youth do not last.
- B. The Gospel of Jesus Christ is everlasting. Eternal.

VI. L-ove

"For God so loved . . . that he gave . . ." (John 3:16).

A. Love is the basis for the good news of the Gospel.

B. God loved so much He gave His Son. Jesus loved so much He gave Himself. We, also, must love (1 John 4:11).

15. How to Find Rest

"Come unto me all ye that labour and are heavy laden, and I will give you rest" (Matt. 11:28).

I. The Person
"Come unto me . . ." (Matt. 11:28).
A. Many are trying to find rest by going on vacations, taking up hobbies, and seeking pleasures and entertainment.
B. Many are trying to find rest by going to doctors, lawyers, friends, and counselors.
C. Jesus Christ is the Person who can give lasting and enduring rest. Other ways and means help but they are ineffective without the Person (Heb. 12:2).

II. The People
"All ye that labour and are heavy laden . . ." (Matt. 11:28).
A. Millions of people today are laden down with sin and guilt.
B. Many Christians are encumbered with doubts, worries, and the cares of life.
C. The "people" includes all who are heavy laden. No one is excluded. Jesus has compassion for every individual (Matt. 9:36).

III. The Promise
"And I will give you rest" (Matt. 11:28).
A. This promise means forgiveness, freedom from bondage and guilt, and rest from fear of death and eternal retribution.
B. This promise releases the Christian from doubts and worry. It brings freedom from the cares and burdens of life.
C. This promise assures us of future and eternal realities. Complete and perfect rest awaits those who place their faith and trust in "The Person, Jesus Christ" (Heb. 4:9-11).

16. How to Follow Christ's Example

"Christ also suffered for us, leaving us an example, that ye should follow his steps" (1 Peter 2:21).

I. He Performed His Father's Will
"Then said I, Lo, I come . . . to do Thy will, O God" (Heb. 10:7).

A. Christ came to do His Father's will willingly and of His own accord.

B. Christians are entreated to do the will of God (Mark 3:35).

II. He Declared His Father's Word
"For I have given unto them the words which thou gavest me" (John 17:8).

A. Christ used the Word of God to defeat Satan in time of temptation.

B. We, too, must use the Word to defeat Satan, to increase our faith, and to point others to Christ.

III. He Walked in His Father's Ways
Jesus *"went about doing good . . . for God was with him" (Acts 10:38).*

A. Jesus forgave sins, healed the sick, and helped all who came to Him for help.

B. We should walk in God's ways, too. A kind word, a smile, the lending of a helping hand, express God through us.

IV. He Fulfilled His Father's Work
"I have finished the work which thou gavest me to do" (John 17:4).

A. Jesus did the work God sent Him to do. He fulfilled His task by dying on the cross for mankind. He was faithful.

B. There is work for each of us to do, also. We must share Christ and seek to win the lost to Him. Let us be faithful to do our Father's work here on earth.

17. How to Get Closer to God

"Draw nigh to God, and he will draw nigh to you" (James 4:8).

I. By Praying to Him.
"When ye pray, believe . . . and ye shall have them" (Mark 11:24).
A. Prayer must be accompanied with desire and faith. The promise is "Ye shall have them."
B. There are prayers of praise, petition, and fellowship. We get closer to God when we use all three of them (Luke 18:1).

II. By Proving His Promises
"Whereby are given unto us exceeding great and precious promises" (2 Peter 1:4).
A. The promises of God are dependable. Not one has ever failed.
B. There are promises in God's Word for every need. We get closer to God when we use them. Our faith grows stronger. Faith pleases God (1 Kings 8:56).

III. By Praising Him
"From the rising of the sun unto the going down of the same the Lord's name is to be praised" (Ps. 113:3).
A. Praise is an effective way to get closer to God. Someone said, "We praised our way through the difficulty." Another, "When you can't pray your way through, praise your way through."
B. Praise pleases God. One cannot complain, find fault, or be discouraged, and truly praise God at the same time (Ps. 34:1).

IV. By Practicing His Presence
"I will not leave you comfortless; I will come to you" (John 14:18).
A. Many Christians often forget, ignore, and disregard God's presence.
B. They should strive, instead, to be aware of God's presence with them continually. He is there, regardless of the circumstances (Heb. 13:5).

V. By Participating in His Work

"I have chosen you . . . that ye should go and bring forth fruit . . ." (John 15:16).

A. To participate means to share, join in, have a hand in, cooperate, get involved. This is what Christians should do where God's work is concerned.

B. When we participate in God's work, we share His friendship (John 15:14).

18. How to Give God First Place

"But seek ye first the kingdom of God, and his righteousness; and all these things shall be added unto you." (Matt 6:33).

I. Put Him Before Pleasure

"Ye have lived in pleasure on the earth, and been wanton . . ." (James 5:5).

A. We live in a pleasure-seeking world. Millions of dollars are spent on entertainment each year.

B. Christians should be faithful to worship God in church attendance, prayer, and the ministry of His Word (Matt. 6:33).

II. Put Him Before Position

"Labour . . . for that meat which endureth unto everlasting life" (John 6:27).

A. Too many people make their jobs too important, but inclement weather or company hinders their church attendance.

B. Position and finances are necessary, but they should be kept in the proper perspective (Matt. 6:33).

III. Put Him Before Popularity

"How can ye believe, which receive honour one of another . . ." (John 5:44).

A. It is natural to want the approval of others. In school, youngsters want to be like the other kids. In the office or factory, it's easy to go along with the crowd.

B. It is most important to have the approval of God. We should be on the offensive by witnessing for Him. He will supply courage and grace (Matt. 6:33).

IV. Put Him Before Possessions

"A man's life consisteth not in the abundance of the things he possesseth" (Luke 12:15).

A. This is a materialistic age. Possessions have captured the hearts of millions. The Scripture warns that the love of money is the root of all evil.

B. God wants our wholehearted devotion. We should be faithful in paying God's tithes and giving our offerings liberally (Matt. 6:33).

19. How to Go A-bout B-eing C-hristian
(The ABC's of Christian Living)

Scripture Reading: Romans 12

"Be not overcome of evil, but overcome evil with good" (Rom. 12:21).

I. A-lways Denounce Sin
"Abhor that which is evil; cleave to that which is good" (Rom. 12:9).
A. Abhor (shrink from, detest) that which is evil. Resist the devil and he will flee (James 4:7).
B. The Christian is to denounce sin everywhere—at work, at play, at home watching TV. Denounce violence, lust (2 Cor. 6:17).
C. Cleave to that which is good. Be so busy doing good and being good that there is no time for evil (James 4:8).

II. B-e Dependable in Serving
"Fervent in spirit; serving the Lord" (Rom. 12:11).
A. Serve with your time. Take time to call, witness, and win the lost to Jesus Christ (Ps. 90:12).
B. Serve with your talent. Everyone can do something for God. Give a kind word, a smile, a helping hand (2 Cor. 6:1).
C. Serve with your treasure. Money is needed to meet church obligations. Money given to God's work is saved (Matt. 6:19-21).

III. C-ontinue Dedication of Self
"Present your bodies a living sacrifice . . ." (Rom. 12:1).
A. Read God's Word. It is a guide, a chart, to show us where to go and what to do (Ps. 119:11).
B. Pray. Be always in the spirit of prayer. We are privileged to commune and fellowship with God (Luke 18:1).
C. Surrender all to God. Live with a yielded-to-God attitude (1 Cor. 6:19-20).

20. How to Grow in Faith

"We . . . thank God . . . that your faith groweth exceedingly" (2 Thess. 1:3).

I. Realize the Purpose of Faith
"He that cometh to God must believe . . ." (Heb. 11:6).
- A. Faith is the way to please God.
- B. Faith is the means by which we receive God (2 Peter 1:9).
- C. Faith is the way to receive blessings from God.
- D. Faith enables us to do things for God.

II. Remember the Promises of Faith
"Whatsoever ye shall ask in prayer, believing, ye shall receive" (Matt. 21:22).
- A. The promises of faith are extensive enough to meet all our needs—physical, mental, and spiritual (Phil. 4:19).
- B. Acquaint yourself with the promises by searching the Scriptures.
- C. Memorize the promises.
- D. Apply the promises to your areas of need.

III. Recognize the Privilege of Faith
"Saved through Faith . . . not of yourselves: it is the gift of God" (Eph. 2:8).
- A. Faith is not merited or earned; it cannot be purchased.
- B. Faith is given to us by God. Simply take it.
- C. Faith is for all—the young and old, rich and poor, black and white.
- D. God is the author and finisher of our faith (Heb. 12:2).

IV. Respond to the Power of Faith
"Kept by the power of God through Faith . . ." (1 Peter 1:5).
- A. God's power is unlimited. He is omnipotent.
- B. Faith releases God's power.
- C. Active faith accomplishes the impossible—removes mountains, lifts burdens, sets men free from the bondage of sin.
- D. Faith is the victory (1 John 5:4).

21. How to Grow Up Spiritually

"But grow in grace, and in the knowledge of our Lord and Savior Jesus Christ" (2 Peter 3:18).

I. Spiritual Baby Stage
"Even as unto babes in Christ" (1 Cor. 3:1).
- A. Babies live to be served. They are concerned only with themselves.
- B. Some Christians are spiritual babies. They need to be filled with the Holy Spirit so they can begin to "grow in grace" (1 Cor. 3:2-3).

II. Spiritual Child Stage
"I write unto you little children, because your sins are forgiven you . . ." (1 John 2:12).
- A. Children are selfish and want their own way. They repeat what they hear, love attention, and want to be praised.
- B. Some Christians are still children spiritually. They need to mature emotionally and in the knowledge of the Lord (Eph. 4:14).

III. Spiritual Youth Stage
"I write unto you, young men, because ye have overcome the wicked one" (1 John 2:13).
- A. Young people often make quick, rash, and unwise choices. They are strong and energetic but are often hindered by feelings of inferiority. Youths need guidance, direction, and purpose.
- B. Many Christians never grow beyond this stage. God wants them to grow spiritually by seeking His guidance, direction, purpose, and strength (2 Peter 3:18).

IV. Spiritual Adult Stage
"I have written unto you fathers, because ye have known him that is from the beginning" (1 John 2:14).
- A. Mature Christians love God and give Him first place in their lives. They are considerate of others and work together in harmony.
- B. Mature Christians live by faith, not according to the dictates of their emotions. They put away childish things (1 Cor. 13:11).

22. How to Have a Happy Home

"If any man will come after me, let him deny himself, and take up his cross, and follow me" (Matt. 16:24).

I. Be Cheerful
"A merry heart doeth good like a medicine" (Prov. 17:22).
- A. There are many drab, cheerless abodes. Depressive homes are unhealthy—physically, mentally, and spiritually.
- B. Our homes should be kept alive with cheer and joy. This goes a long way toward having a happy home (Phil. 4:4).

II. Be Courteous
"Be courteous" (1 Peter 3:8).
- A. Some people are respectful and polite at work and at church. They are courteous to friends and strangers but they show little, if any, respect to their companion, the one who stands by them in sickness and hardship.
- B. Little courtesies are important. Open the door for your wife. Never criticize your husband in public. Say "Thank you" to your children (Rom. 12:10).

III. Be Cooperative
"As workers together with him" (2 Cor. 6:1).
- A. "Let's go together"—we are workers together for the mutual good of all. A "you-go-your-way-and-I'll-go-mine" attitude widens the gap.
- B. Be loyal. Never criticize, nor allow criticism, of your family. Keep family secrets. Keep the intimate a sacred trust (1 Peter 3:8-9).

IV. Be Consistent
"Having the same love, being of one accord" (Phil. 2:2).
- A. Firmness, coherence, and discipline are necessary where children are concerned. Limits must be set and enforced by both parents.
- B. If children are to obey God later in life, they must learn to obey their parents while young.
- C. Children need the security that parents' faith, firmness, and discipline (with reason) brings (Eph. 6:1-4).

V. Be Christian

"As ye have . . . received Christ . . . so walk ye in him" (Col. 2:6).

A. Don't be afraid to tell your children, your husband/wife, "I love you." They may know it, but they need to hear it from you.

B. Let love rule and lead the way. Everyone makes mistakes. Forgive and forget, and you're well on your way to having a happy home.

C. Give God first place (Matt. 6:33).

23. How to H-O-P-E in God

"Hope thou in God" (Ps. 42:5).

I. H-eritage
"Made heirs according to the hope of eternal life" (Titus 3:7).
- A. Heritage—"that which is inherited; the lot, condition, or status into which one is born" (Webster).
- B. Being justified by faith through Jesus Christ gives us the hope of eternal life, making us heirs of God and joint-heirs with Jesus Christ (Rom. 8:16-17).

II. O-ptimism
"Happy is he . . . whose hope is in the Lord his God" (Ps. 146:5).
- A. Optimism—"an inclination to put the most favorable construction upon actions and happenings, or anticipate the best possible outcome" (Webster).
- B. Hope brings optimism and good cheer. Optimism looks for and expects the best (Rom. 8:28).

III. P-atience
"Remembering . . . your . . . patience of hope in our Lord Jesus Christ" (1 Thess. 1:3).
- A. Most Christians need more patience.
- B. Patience of hope is developed through affliction, trial, and temptation—with the help of the Lord (1 Peter 5:10).

IV. E-ternal Life
"In hope of eternal life, which God . . . promised . . ." (Titus 1:2).
- A. Hope means "happy expectation." The Christian has the hope, the "happy expectation," of eternal life.
- B. We must set our affections on things above so we can claim the treasures laid up for us in heaven (Col. 1:5).

24. How to Increase Your Faith

"The apostles said unto the Lord, Increase our faith" (Luke 17:5).

I. Think Faith

"Let this mind be in you, which was also in Christ Jesus" (Phil. 2:5).

A. Negative thinking must be discarded. It is displeasing to God.

B. Fill your mind with thoughts of praise and assurance. Think faith thoughts—thoughts about God's presence and good will toward others.

II. Hear Faith

"He that heareth . . . and believeth . . . hath everlasting life" (John 5:24).

A. We listen to many voices—voices of newscasters (who relay to us mostly bad news), voices of criticism, doubts.

B. Faith is increased as we listen to the good, pure, and positive.

C. Listen to the voice of God. He speaks when we become quiet and receptive (Ps. 46:10).

III. See Faith

"Looking unto Jesus the author and finisher of our faith" (Heb. 12:2).

A. Many have their eyes on temporal things—they desire to obtain houses, land, automobiles, money.

B. Christians must keep their eyes on Christ, they must be concerned with giving Him first place in their lives, and winning the lost.

IV. Talk Faith

"Talk ye of all his wondrous works" (Ps. 105:2).

A. Many women talk about fashions, styles, neighbors, friends.

B. Many men talk about the news, money, cars, houses, jobs.

C. All Christians should talk about the things of God—His salvation, love, peace, blessings.

V. Work Your Faith

"I will shew thee my faith by my works" (James 2:18).

A. Active faith is effective.

B. Your faith grows as you exercise it. Work your faith, then it works for you.

C. Jesus condemned the Pharisees when He said, "For they say and do not" (Matt. 23:3). He wants workers, not talkers.

VI. Walk By Faith
"We walk by faith, not by sight" (2 Cor. 5:7).

A. Walk by faith in daily living—in work, and in play.
B. Walk by faith in the hour of trial and temptation.
C. Walk by faith when the sun is shining.
D. Walking by faith increases our faith and brings God's approval.

25. How to Live Happily

"And now abideth faith, hope, charity . . ." (1 Cor. 13:13).

I. Fear Not (Faith)

"Fear not: believe only . . ." (Luke 8:50).

A. Jairus' daughter was raised from the dead because of Jairus' faith. Jesus said, "Fear not, only believe."

B. Fear hinders the happy Christian life—fear of losing one's job, fear of old age, fear of the future, fear of death.

C. Faith is the answer, the cure, the antidote for fear. Faith is the victory (1 John 5:4).

II. Faint Not (Hope)

"We shall reap, if we faint not" (Gal. 6:9).

A. Discouragement can defeat believers. Satan uses discouragement to cause Christians to give up.

B. Satan discourages us with affliction, financial difficulties, and misunderstandings.

C. Hope in God overcomes discouragement. We hope in God through prayer and God's Word, positive thinking, and looking for the good (Ps. 146:5).

III. Fret Not (Love)

"Fret not thyself because of evildoers . . ." (Ps. 37:1).

A. Fretting causes unhappiness. Christians often fret about their neighbors, mates, friends, job, church, the world.

B. Love is the cure for fretting. Love covers a multitude of sins. The more of God's love one has, the less fretting one will do (1 Peter 4:8).

C. Jesus Christ died willingly for you and me. He gave His life without complaining, because He loved so much. Love makes the difference (1 John 3:16).

26. How to Keep from Discouragement

"But they that wait upon the Lord shall renew their strength; they shall mount up with wings as eagles; they shall run, and not be weary; and they shall walk, and not faint" (Isa. 40:31).

I. Remember What God Has Done
"The Lord hath done great things for us . . ." (Ps. 126:3).

A. God gave His Son to die for our sins. Jesus gave Himself that we might be cleansed from all unrighteousness.

B. The skeptic declares that God has done nothing for him, that he has gotten everything through his own power.

C. The man of faith knows that all good things come from above. Strength, health, and life itself are gifts from the good hand of God (James 1:17).

II. Recognize What God Is Doing
"This is the Lord's doing, and it is marvelous in our eyes" (Matt. 21:42).

A. God is alive today. He is working in the lives of those who let Him. We should be aware of His power and presence.

B. Christians should be excited about what God is doing. They should not become complacent and unconcerned about God's work.

C. We can keep from discouragement by thinking about what God is doing presently. A positive attitude will help us to see the good and expect the best (Phil. 4:4).

III. Rejoice About What God Will Do
"Rejoice: for the Lord will do great things" (Joel 2:21).

A. We must face the future with an attitude of faith. God has promised to help us in time of need, and to give strength and courage for all our tomorrows.

B. We are promised eternity with the Lord. He has prepared wonderful things for those who trust Him (Rev. 21:4).

C. We can keep from being discouraged by thinking of what God has promised and will do.

27. How to Know What God Will Do

"For it is God which worketh in you both to will and to do of his good pleasure" (Phil. 2:13).

I. Safety

"I will be with him in trouble; I will deliver him . . ." (Ps. 91:15).

A. Today's world is filled with danger and turmoil. Many streets and neighborhoods are unsafe.

B. Many depend on weapons and power for safety, but the Christian can depend upon the Lord to guard and protect him (Prov. 29:25).

II. Strength

"I will strengthen thee" (Isa. 41:10).

A. God has promised strength for each day.

B. Paul declared, "When I am weak, then am I strong," for he especially depended on the Lord when he was weak in himself.

C. God's promises include strength to endure trials, temptations, and persecution. His grace is sufficient (Ps. 27:1).

III. Security

"When thou passest through the waters, I will be with thee" (Isa. 43:2).

A. Many seek security through accumulating large bank accounts, insurance, stocks, bonds, houses, and land.

B. Real security is found only in Christ. He will never leave nor forsake us (Job 11:18).

IV. Serenity

"I will give you rest" (Matt. 11:28).

A. We find rest, peace, and freedom from guilt when we accept Christ as Savior and are received into the family of God.

B. The hope of spending eternity with Christ brings peace and rest. We no longer fear the future, death, or the judgment (Ps. 37:7).

V. Service

"I will make you fishers of men" (Matt. 4:19).

A. As we follow Christ, we find a place of service by doing those things that are pleasing in His sight.

B. We serve Him by witnessing, sharing, praying, and by becoming fishers of men (Ps. 101:6).

28. How to Learn About Christ

"God . . . hath . . . spoken unto us by his Son, whom he hath appointed heir of all things, by whom also he made the worlds" (Heb. 1:1-2).

I. Humility—by His Birth
"And she brought forth her first born son . . . and laid him in a manger" (Luke 2:7).
A. The birth of Jesus Christ, the Son of God, in the little town of Bethlehem is a classic example of humility.
B. Christ wants us to be humble, too—to love the poor as well as the rich, the uneducated as well as the educated (James 4:10).

II. Faith—by His Life
"I must work the works of him that sent me . . ." (John 9:4).
A. Christ epitomized the life of faith. His touch brought healing, comfort, and peace to needy lives.
B. We too must live our faith, working, witnessing, and winning (James 2:24).

III. Love—by His Death
"The Son of God . . . loved me, and gave himself for me" (Gal. 2:20).
A. Christ's love for sinful men sent Him to the cross. He died for our sanctification (Heb. 13:12).
B. We are to love with words of kindness, helpfulness, attitudes of good will, and by sharing the Good News of the gospel with others (John 13:34).

IV. Life—by His Resurrection
"I am the resurrection and the life" (John 11:25).
A. Christ arose from the dead, triumphant over death, hell, and the grave. He is alive forevermore (Rev. 1:18).
B. Christ wants us to have life, too. Those who repent and believe may have eternal life.

V. Hope—by His Ascension
"I will come again, and receive you unto myself" (John 14:3).

A. Christ ascended to heaven to prepare a place for those who love Him. He is coming again to receive them unto Himself.
B. The hope of the Christian is eternal life. Believers will be caught up to be together with loved ones gone on before. In heaven they will live with the Lord forever (1 Thess. 4:17).

29. How to Live by Faith

"The just shall live by faith" (Gal. 3:11).

I. Start the Venture of Faith

"Faith is . . . the evidence of things not seen" (Heb. 11:1).

A. Venture means—"to dare, to risk, to undertake." But when we begin the venture of faith, we have everything to gain and nothing to lose.

B. When we begin to live by faith, God sends blessings we never dreamed possible. Miracles begin to happen.

C. Courage is needed to accept the challenge.

II. Stress the Value of Faith

"Above all, taking the shield of faith . . ." (Eph. 6:16).

A. Faith is valuable because it pleases God.

B. Faith is the means by which we receive salvation (Eph. 2:8).

C. Faith brings healing, financial help, and numerous other blessings.

D. Faith keeps us steadfast and secure, and helps us to resist Satan.

III. Share the Vision of Faith

"Looking unto Jesus the author and finisher of our faith" (Heb. 12:2).

A. *Vision* is the ability "to direct the eyes, to discern, distinguish, discover."

B. Faith fosters a positive outlook.

C. The vision of faith discovers otherwise unseen possibilities and opportunities.

D. Faith also causes us to share our confidence that God will keep His promises.

IV. Sound the Victory of Faith

"This is the victory . . . even our faith" (1 John 5:4).

A. Faith always brings the victory. Our finite powers are linked to God's infinite resources.

B. Recognizing victories strengthens one's own faith.

C. Sharing our victories inspires the faith of others. Faith is contagious.

D. God should always be praised and glorified, for He deserves our continual praise (Heb. 13:15).

30. How to Make C-H-R-I-S-T Your Life

Scripture Reading: Colossians 3:1-4

"When Christ, who is our life, shall appear, then shall ye also appear with him in glory" (Col. 3:4).

I. C-enter
"Christ is all, and in all" (Col. 3:11b).
A. Every life must have a center around which to build. Some build their lives around material wealth, some around pleasure, and some around other people.
B. Successful lives are built around Christ. When storms arise, when waves roll high, Christ is steadfast and unmovable.

II. H-ope
"Lord Jesus Christ, which is our hope" (1 Tim. 1:1b).
A. Many place their hope in political power, atomic energy, education, scientific achievement, position.
B. Jesus Christ is the only hope for the world, the church, the individual. He can lift up the depressed, the burdened, the tempted (Ps. 71:5).

III. R-edeemer
"Being justified . . . through the redemption that is in Christ Jesus" (Rom. 3:24).
A. Silver and gold cannot buy salvation. Houses and lands cannot redeem a soul.
B. By His death on the cross, Jesus Christ redeemed (purchased, bought back) those who repent and believe in Him (1 Peter 1:18-21).

IV. I-nstructor
"I will instruct thee and teach thee . . ." (Ps. 32:8).
A. To receive an education one must work, study, apply himself, use the text books, listen to the teacher.
B. Christ is the Heavenly Instructor. Read the text (the Bible), attend church faithfully, listen to the teacher (the Lord) (2 Tim. 2:15).

V. S-trength
"The Lord is the strength of my life" (Ps. 27:1).

A. Strength is needed to live in today's world. There are constant threats of war, strife, trouble, turmoil.
B. Christ gives strength. He is omnipotent, able to show His power in every situation (Isa. 46:4).

VI. T-rust

"Commit thy way unto the Lord; trust also in him" (Ps. 37:5).

A. Some trust in uncertain riches; some, achievements; some, other people.
B. Trust in the Lord. He is the only One who never fails (1 Cor. 2:5).

31. How to Praise the Lord

"Let everything that hath breath praise the Lord" (Ps. 150:6).

I. Praise Him for Past Blessings
"I will praise thy name; for thou hast done wonderful things" (Isa. 25:1).

A. Recall past blessings—remember answers to prayer, miracles that took place. Recall the small details and circumstances surrounding your prayers.

B. Praise the Lord. Be grateful, and give thanks for the many blessings of the past.

C. Remembering God's past blessings and answers to prayer inspires faith and brings new hope.

II. Praise Him for Present Blessings
"Every day will I bless thee; and . . . praise thy name" (Ps. 145:2).

A. Some think they have nothing to praise the Lord for, but they need to look for the good in their lives.

B. Make a list—write down the blessings that are yours: life, salvation, family, church, home, etc.

C. Praise brings a positive outlook, a desire to reach out, to inspire, to help, to share with others about the goodness of Christ.

III. Praise Him for Potential Blessings
"Be glad and rejoice: for the Lord will do great things" (Joel 2:21).

A. Expect the best. According to your faith, so be it.

B. Look to the future with faith and anticipation. Keep seeking, reaching, and expecting the highest and best.

C. Praise the Lord—for what He is going to do. Work to help bring it to pass. Set goals for yourself. The Lord can bring the impossible to pass.

32. How to Measure God's Love

"Being rooted and grounded in love . . . may [you] be able to comprehend . . . what is the breadth, and length, and depth, and height" (Eph. 3:17-18).

I. God's Love Reaches Up
His great love made us "sit together in heavenly places" (Eph. 2:4-6).

A. God's love reaches higher than the tallest mountain, the highest star. When we love, heaven is brought near. God is close because He is love.

B. Love reaches those who climb the social ladder, kings and presidents. Saturated with God's love, all believers become one in Christ Jesus (1 John 5:2).

II. God's Love Reaches Down
"Thou hast in love to my soul delivered it from the pit of corruption" (Isa. 38:17).

A. God's love reaches down into the slums, the ghetto, skid row, the lowest of the low. It reaches down to the drunkard, gambler, prostitute, thief, liar.

B. His love penetrates deeper than the stain of sin. All who repent and believe may be lifted out of the miry clay of sin.

III. God's Love Reaches In
"His love is perfected in us" (1 John 4:12).

A. God's love reaches into the heart and soul to mellow, freshen, enrich, purify, and heal. It breaks down evil, casts out fear, and perfects the spirit (1 John 4:18).

B. God is love—within us. He brings strength, courage, kindness, patience, compassion, and forgiveness.

IV. God's Love Reaches Out
"God so loved the world . . . that whosoever believeth . . . should not perish" (John 3:16).

A. God's love reaches out to the far corners of the earth. There is no limit to His reach. It solves problems, lifts burdens, and forgives sins on the mission fields.

B. God's love reaches out through our prayers to our loved ones far and near and to His people around the world.

V. God's Love Reaches Through

Nothing "shall be able to separate us from the love of God" (Rom. 8:39).

A. There is no defense against God's love. It can penetrate any situation. It reaches through prison walls, walls of resentment and strife—to victory.

B. Love reaches through darkness, trial, suffering, sorrow, bereavement, and death, to bring eternal life.

33. How to Profit by Praise

"From the rising of the sun unto the going down of the same the Lord's name is to be praised" (Ps. 113:3).

I. Praise Activates Faith

"In God I will praise his word, in God I have put my trust" (Ps. 56:4).

A. Praising the Lord may require a step of faith. One may not feel like praising the Lord, but to do so generates and activates faith.

B. Praising God overrides doubts and says, "I believe God, anyhow."

C. Praising God breaks down Satan's defenses.

II. Praise Stimulates Hope

"Hope thou in God: for I shall yet praise him . . ." (Ps. 42:5).

A. Praising the Lord automatically and necessarily brings one to hope in God. Hope follows praise.

B. Praising God is a positive step, an upward look, a declaration of faith. These things bring hope into focus.

C. Jesus Christ is the hope of the world. Money, power, and war cannot meet our needs, but He can.

III. Praise Increases Love

"Let them also that love thy name be joyful with thee" (Ps. 5:11).

A. It is difficult to praise the Lord and hold a grudge at the same time. Hostility and resentment and praise do not go together.

B. When we praise the Lord, He becomes the object of our affection, thus increasing our love toward Him and others.

C. The angels of God and the redeemed of all ages shall praise God eternally (Rev. 19:1).

to Pray As Jesus Did

ʒ: Matthew 26:36-45

ısus with them unto a place called Gethsemane,
the disciples, Sit ye here, while I go and pray
yonder" (Matt. 26:36).

I. He Prayed Alone
"And again he went away, and prayed . . ." (Mark 14:39; Luke 22:41; Matt. 26:39).
A. Jesus often communed alone with God on the mountainside. He prayed alone when He was facing the most crucial time of His life.
B. It is good to pray with other Christians, but there are times, perhaps crucial times, when we should be alone with God in the prayer closet (Matt. 6:6).

II. He Prayed With Humility
"He . . . kneeled down, and prayed" (Luke 22:41; Mark 14:35; Matt. 26:39).
A. Jesus was humble. His life, His birth, and death on the cross exemplify this.
B. We must humble ourselves before God as we pray (1 Peter 5:5-6).

III. He Prayed Earnestly
"And being in agony he prayed more earnestly" (Luke 22:44).
A. Jesus was experiencing the greatest struggle of His life. The hope and life of the world were at stake.
B. In times of trouble and trial, every Christian must pray more earnestly.

IV. He Prayed Persistently
"And again he went away, and prayed . . ." (Mark 14:39).
A. Jesus did not stop short. He kept praying until He was assured of victory.
B. We must prevail by taking our burdens to the Lord until we are assured He has heard.

V. He Prayed with Submission
"O my Father . . . thy will be done" (Matt. 26:42; Mark 14:36; Luke 22:42).
A. Jesus resigned Himself to the Father's will.
B. We should pray with submission. Total yieldedness to God brings the victory.

35. How to Receive God's Help

Scripture Reading: Psalm 91

"Because he hath set his love upon me, therefore will I deliver him" (Ps. 91:14).

I. God's Presence

"He . . . shall abide under the shadow of the Almighty" (Ps. 91:1).

A. Fellowship awaits us in the presence of God. His children enjoy a family relationship. They feel safe, secure, and at ease.

B. We should practice God's presence. He is with us every day, hour, and moment (Heb. 13:5).

II. God's Power

"He is my refuge and fortress . . . surely he shall deliver thee . . ." (Ps. 91:2-4).

A. God is omnipotent. His great power created the heavens and the earth.

B. He is abundantly able to meet all our needs. He can change circumstances and people. He can keep us secure in Him (2 Tim. 1:12).

III. God's Providence

"Thou shalt not be afraid . . . it shall not come nigh thee . . . thine eyes shalt . . . see the reward of the wicked" (Ps. 91:5-8).

A. Providence means "the act of providing." It is "divine guidance, through His loving care and intervention."

B. God provides an escape from trial and temptation. He directs and intervenes in unusual ways (Heb. 13:8).

IV. God's Protection

"There shall no evil befall thee. . . . He shall give his angels charge over thee . . ." (Ps. 91:10-11; Ps. 91:9-13).

A. Distance is no problem with God.

B. As we pray He reaches down to protect our families, loved ones, missionaries, and friends (Heb. 13:6).

V. God's Promises

"I will be with him in trouble; I will deliver him and honour him" (Ps. 91:15; Ps. 91:14-16).

A. The promises of God are great and many. They cannot fail because God cannot fail.

B. We can claim His promises only as we meet His condition—setting "our love on" Him (Heb. 10:23).

36. How to Recognize God's Blessings

Scripture Reading: Numbers 6:22-27

"And I will bless them" (Num. 6:27).

I. Protective Care
"The Lord bless thee, and keep thee" (Num. 6:24).
- A. This generation is the most dangerous, reckless, lawless in the history of the world.
- B. God promises to bless those who walk in His statutes and keep His commandments with protective care.
- C. God is the same yesterday, today, and forever (Heb. 13:8).

II. Paternal Love
"The Lord make his face shine upon thee, and be gracious unto thee" (Num. 6:25).
- A. The Lord's favor and love have always been extended to His people (Lev. 26:12).
- B. God loves His children with a paternal love; He is gracious, kind, and understanding.
- C. We become His children by confessing our sins, trusting Him to forgive and cleanse us from unrighteousness (1 John 1:9).

III. Peaceful Approbation
"The Lord lift up his countenance upon thee, and give thee peace" (Num. 6:26).
- A. The blessing of peace was given to the children of Israel when they obeyed God (Lev. 26:6).
- B. The blessing of peace will be bestowed upon those who keep their minds stayed on the Lord (Isa. 26:3).
- C. In today's world of strife, let us thank God for His blessing of peaceful approbation.

37. How to Recognize the Spirit-Filled

"But be filled with the Spirit" (Eph. 5:18).

I. They Worship in the Spirit
"Worship him in Spirit and in truth" (John 4:24).
   A. Spirit-filled Christians are not in bondage to a form of godliness; they are not fanatics or daydreamers. They are not bound by social pressures or by the spirit of the age.
   B. Spirit-filled Christians worship with the anointing of God and the witness of the Holy Spirit.

II. They Work Together in Unity
"Continuing daily with one accord" (Acts 2:46).
   A. Spirit-filled Christians do not work against one another. They are in harmony—no resentments, frictions, or divisions.
   B. They are concerned about getting God's work accomplished. Christians work together in unity when they love God and one another (Eph. 4:3).

III. They Are Willing to Forgive Others
"Forbearing . . . and forgiving one another" (Col. 3:13).
   A. Spirit-filled Christians make mistakes and blunders just like everyone else, but they possess a forgiving spirit. They do not hold resentments. As God forgave them, so they forgive others.
   B. Forgiveness lifts burdens, brings joy and peace to mind and soul (Matt. 6:14-15).

IV. They Walk in Divine Love
"And walk in love, as Christ also hath loved us" (Eph. 5:2).
   A. God's love is implanted in the heart by God Himself and it works its way out to bless others.
   B. When Christians surrender themselves to God, they are cleansed of sinful attitudes, hatred, and strife, and are filled with the Holy Spirit of love.

V. They Witness to the Lost

"And ye shall be witnesses unto me" (Acts 1:8).

A. Spirit-filled Christians welcome opportunities to share what Christ means to them with others. Witnessing is a natural consequence of this infilling.

B. They believe they are indebted to give the gospel to others in the same measure they received it (Rom. 1:14-16).

38. How to Recognize True Value

"Chosen of God, and precious" (1 Peter 2:4).

I. Precious—the Blood of Christ
"Ye are . . . redeemed with the precious blood of Christ" (1 Peter 1:18-19).
A. Christ paid the penalty for sin by His death on the cross.
B. The blood of Christ is life. It redeems (buys back, purchases) our salvation. All who repent, believe, and accept Him as Savior have eternal life.

II. Precious—the Promises of God
"Given unto us exceeding great and precious promises" (2 Peter 1:4).
A. The promises are precious because they are from God's Word and can be depended on. They are of great value and highly esteemed (Num. 23:19).
B. The promises are for our use. They bring salvation, healing, comfort, strength, eternal life (John 5:24).

III. Precious—the Trial of Faith
"The trial of your faith, being much more precious than of gold . . ." (1 Peter 1:7).
A. God allows trials in our lives to strengthen our faith, to teach us lessons we need to learn, and to test our determination to be true to Him.
B. Trials take us deeper with God and make us greater blessings for God. The greater the trial and testing we must go through, the stronger our faith becomes. Job, Daniel, the three Hebrew children are examples (1 Peter 4:12).

IV. Precious—the Death of Christians
"Precious in the sight of the Lord is the death of his saints" (Ps. 116:15).
A. The death of saints is precious because God wants them to be with Him. He promotes them from an earthly house to a building of God, not made with hands (2 Cor. 5:1).
B. Christians should not fear death, but they should declare with Paul that to live is Christ but to die is gain (Phil. 1:21).

39. How to Tame Tension

Scripture Reading: Matthew 6:25-34

"Take therefore no [anxious] thought for the morrow" (Matt. 6:34).

I. Concentrate on Relaxing Influences
"Whatsoever things are lovely . . . think on these things" (Phil. 4:8).
A. Fellowship with nature, God's creation—the hills, valleys, streams. This is relaxing.
B. Listen to music by the great masters and the soothing hymns of the church.
C. Meditate on God's promises. Pray and fellowship with the Lord.

II. Cultivate a Sense of Humor
"A merry heart doeth good like a medicine" (Prov. 17:22).
A. Don't take yourself too seriously. See the humorous side of life.
B. Learn to laugh at your mistakes and blunders. Everyone makes them.
C. Laugh *at* situations and circumstances and *with* people.

III. Control Extravagant Ambitions
"Seek ye first the kingdom of God . . . these things shall be added unto you" (Matt. 6:33).
A. Pace yourself. Know your limitations.
B. Learn to be yourself, to do what God wants, no more, no less.
C. Ambition if not controlled can lead to unhappiness and strain.

IV. Cooperate with the Inevitable
"All things work together for good to them who love God . . ." (Rom. 8:28).
A. Accept situations that you cannot change.
B. Jesus lived a relaxed life; He did not fret about difficult situations but turned impossibilities into opportunities.

V. Consistently Trust in the Lord

"Trust in him at all times" (Ps. 62:8).

A. Be aware that God is with you always. Practice the presence of God.

B. Remember, you are linked to omnipotence. You are not meeting life's demands alone.

C. Yield yourself to His will and way. Let Him do His work through you.

40. How to Share the Good Shepherd's Gifts

Scripture Reading: Psalm 23

"I am the good shepherd: the good shepherd giveth his life for the sheep" (John 10:11).

I. He Gives Satisfaction
"The Lord is my shepherd; I shall not want" (Ps. 23:1).
A. Sheep do not worry about tomorrow.
B. Neither should we want or worry about the future. The Lord has promised to supply all our needs (Phil. 4:9).

II. He Gives Serenity
"He maketh me to lie down in green pastures; he leadeth me beside the still waters" (Ps. 23:2).
A. When the sheep become hot and tired, the shepherd makes them lie down in cool, soft pasture to rest.
B. Sheep are afraid of swift running water and drink only from still waters.
C. Sometimes we must be drawn aside to rest, meditate, and pray. The Lord gives us serenity.

III. He Gives Strength
"He restoreth my soul" (Ps. 23:3).
A. Sheep are weak, have poor sight, and a poor sense of direction.
B. The Lord restores our strength when we are wounded by trials or cut deeply by sorrow.
C. He leads us carefully when the way is rugged and dark.

IV. He Gives Safety
"I will fear no evil; for thou art with me" (Ps. 23:4).
A. In David's time, the shepherd used a rod (a heavy club, two to three feet long) to protect the sheep from wild animals, and a staff (about eight feet long with a crook at the end) to reach the sheep that fell into ditches or crevices.
B. The Lord protects us from evil and lifts us up when we fall.

V. He Gives Sustenance
"Thou preparest a table before me . . ." (Ps. 23:5).
A. The shepherd dug up the poisonous plants and burned

them—literally preparing a "table" for the sheep. He applied healing oil to the sheep's wounds.

B. The cleansing, healing oil of the Holy Spirit is applied to our hearts when we are hurt or wounded.

VI. He Gives Security

"I will dwell in the house of the Lord for ever" (Ps. 23:6).

A. Everyone needs security.

B. Knowing that the Lord is preparing a home for us in heaven gives us security. Where He is, there we may be also (John 14:1-3).

41. How to Share Your Faith

"In all things showing thyself a pattern of good works" (Titus 2:7).

I. Be Friendly
"A man that hath friends must shew himself friendly" (Prov. 18:24).
- A. Christ is a never-failing friend, one "that sticketh closer than a brother."
- B. We, too, must be friendly, cordial, hospitable, and warm-hearted if we are to bring others to a saving knowledge of Jesus Christ.

II. Be Forgiving
"Forgiving one another ... as God ... hath forgiven you" (Eph. 4:32).
- A. Christ is forgiving. He remembers our sins no more when we repent and believe (Heb. 10:17).
- B. We must forgive others, holding no resentments. If we do not forgive others, God will not forgive us (Matt. 6:14-15).
- C. We need to forgive ourselves, also.

III. Be Fearless
"Fear ye not, neither be afraid ... ye are even my witnesses" (Isa. 44:8).
- A. Christ was never afraid. He faced opposition with boldness and courage. His message of salvation came through loud and clear.
- B. We, too, should serve the Lord with dauntless courage, and should always be ready to witness to the saving power of Jesus Christ.

IV. Be Fervent
"Fervent in spirit: serving the Lord" (Rom. 12:11).
- A. Christ was not discouraged, despondent, or depressed. He taught the great truths of His salvation with enthusiasm and zeal.
- B. We, too, should be fervent in spirit as we share Christ with others, help the needy, and feed the hungry.

V. Be Faithful
"Be thou faithful unto death, and I will give thee a crown of life" (Rev. 2:10).

A. Jesus was devoted to the task of helping, hea.
serving others. He was faithful unto death, thus n
salvation possible for all mankind.
B. We should be faithful to the tasks that have been set before
us. A crown of life awaits those who are faithful.

to Use Your Five
tual Senses

ing, and aking

God, which is in thee . . ." (2 Tim. 1:6).

on

s no vision, the people perish" (Prov. 29:18).

of vision is developed by looking for the good, not the bad. We find what we are looking for.

B. Develop this sense by seeing the needs of others, lending a helping hand, witnessing and winning the unsaved to Jesus Christ (Acts 26:19-20).

II. Sense of Hearing

"So then faith cometh by hearing, and hearing by the word of God" (Rom. 10:17).

A. We listen to many voices—voices of friends, neighbors, loved ones; voices on radio, and television. We hear planes overhead, the grate of traffic, and the humming of machines.

B. We should listen carefully for the voice of God. He speaks through His Word, His Holy Spirit, and through daily circumstances (Rom. 8:16).

III. Sense of Smell

"An odour of a sweet smell, a sacrifice . . . wellpleasing to God" (Phil. 4:18).

A. This spiritual sense is developed by our sacrifice for God— for His church, His cause and purpose.

B. Christ is spoken of as the Rose of Sharon and the Lily of the Valley (Song of Sol. 2:1). This sweet-smelling savor becomes a reality when we accept Him as Savior and Lord.

IV. Sense of Taste

"O taste and see that the Lord is good" (Ps. 34:8).

A. When one partakes of food, it actually becomes a part of one.

B. When we surrender ourselves to God, partake of His living Word by faith, He comes into our hearts to abide with us. We are one together with the Lord (John 17:23).

V. Sense of Touch

"If I may but touch the hem of his garment, I shall be whole" (Matt. 9:21).

A. We may touch Him in behalf of others—for their salvation, strength, healing, financial assistance.
B. He will touch us—giving help and strength (physical, mental, and spiritual) when we need it. "According to your faith" (Matt. 9:29).

43. How to Visualize the C-H-U-R-C-H

Scripture Reading: Colossians 1:13-20

"He is the head of the body, the church" (Col. 1:18).

I. C-hrist-centered
"Christ is the head of the church" (Eph. 5:23).
  - A. Churches, like individuals, may become self-centered. If so, their outreach and growth is stunted.
  - B. The church should be Christ-centered, not program-centered. It should not be socially or financially controlled.

II. H-oly in nature
"That he might sanctify and cleanse it . . ." (Eph. 5:26).
  - A. Holy—"Set apart for the worship of God: hallowed; sacred" (Webster).
  - B. The church is not the place for entertainment, social gatherings, or money-raising schemes; the church should be set apart to glorify God in sacred worship.

III. U-niversal in scope
"As Christ also loved the church . . ." (Eph. 5:25).
  - A. The church goes beyond denominational boundaries and includes all born-again Christians.
  - B. The church also exceeds racial and geographical boundaries to win all peoples to Christ.

IV. R-evived in spirit
"But nourisheth and cherisheth it . . ." (Eph. 5:29).
  - A. Many churches have become spiritually lukewarm. They are lean, undernourished, powerless, and lifeless.
  - B. The church should be fervent in spirit, alive unto God, spiritually well-fed and nourished in the faith.

V. C-onsistent in character
"As the church is subject unto Christ . . ." (Eph. 5:24).
  - A. While some churches have resorted to extreme fanaticism, others have resorted to a mere form of godliness while denying God's power.
  - B. The church should be found in the center of God's highway, not in a ditch on the side of the road.

VI. H-eaven-bound

"That he might present it to himself . . ." (Eph. 5:27).

A. The church, which is the body of Christ, will at last be forever with the Lord.

B. The church should be faithful and diligent to the tasks set before it, for the coming of the Lord draweth nigh.

44. How to Utilize God's L-O-V-E

"Charity never faileth" (1 Cor. 13:8).

I. L-ook for the Best in Others
"Love worketh no ill to his neighbor" (Rom. 13:10).

A. Everyone makes mistakes. Everyone has faults. There is also good in everyone. We usually find what we are looking for in people—good or bad.

B. Many look for the worst. They search for faults, building themselves up by tearing others down.

C. Love is a positive attitude. It reaches for the highest and the best.

II. O-ffer Christ's Love to Others
"Owe no man any thing, but to love one another" (Rom. 13:8).

A. Christ loved so much he laid down His life for the lost world (1 John 4:10-11).

B. Love for others gives the Christian assurance that he belongs to God and has eternal life (1 John 3:14).

C. Love for others should not only be in words but in deed and in truth (1 John 3:17-18).

III. V-isualize what Christ Can Do for Others
"Charity shall cover the multitude of sins" (1 Peter 4:8).

A. Love sees possibilities, hope, and help for all people through Christ.

B. Love knows that, by Christ's power, every person can be a blessing.

C. Love acts on possibilities. It takes steps to win others to Christ by prayer, faith, good deeds, and witnessing.

IV. E-xemplify the Spirit of Christ to Others
"Be kindly affectioned one to another with brotherly love" (Rom. 12:10).

A. Christ was kind, compassionate, and understanding.

B. Love emulates Christ. We are to manifest His Spirit each day.

C. Others will respond to the Spirit of Christ when they see the fruits of the Spirit in us (Gal. 5:22-23).

45. How to Walk As Christians

"If we walk in the light as he is in the light . . . we have fellowship one with another, and the blood of Jesus Christ His Son cleanseth us from all sin" (1 John 1:7).

I. Walk in Newness of Life
"Even so we also should walk in newness of life" (Rom. 6:4).
- A. A Christian is a new creature. He is born again. Old things are passed away; behold, all things are become new. (2 Cor. 5:17)
- B. A new Christian should have new friends, new ways, and new places to go.
- C. Christians should have a new life, new love, new joy, new faith, new hope.

II. Walk in the Spirit
"This I say then, walk in the Spirit . . ." (Gal. 5:16).
- A. To walk in the Spirit, one must be filled with the Spirit.
- B. To walk in the Spirit, one must be Christlike, ready to lend a helping hand to those in need.

III. Walk in Truth
"My children walk in truth" (3 John 4).
- A. Jesus called Himself the Truth. We must live honestly.
- B. Walk in truth, doing the things Jesus has bidden us do.

IV. Walk in Wisdom
"Walk in wisdom . . . redeeming the time" (Col. 4:5).
- A. Christians should use wisdom in working for God and the church.
- B. Believers should use wisdom in spending their time, talent, and treasure (James 1:5).

V. Walk in Divine Love
"And walk in love, as Christ also hath loved us . . ." (Eph. 5:2).
- A. Christians should give God first place in their lives because they love Him.
- B. Christians should love one another as Christ has commanded. They should be kind and understanding.

VI. Walk by Faith

"For we walk by faith, not by sight" (2 Cor. 5:7).

A. "Not by sight"—it is sometimes difficult to see beyond the mountains that loom before us on life's highway. We cannot always see, feel, know, or understand God's leadings.

B. "Walk by faith"—it takes faith to find God. It takes faith to keep our eyes on Him. Faith is the victory.

46. How to Walk in the L-I-G-H-T

"But if we walk in the light, as he is in the light, we have fellowship one with another, and the blood of Jesus Christ his Son cleanseth us from all sin" (1 John 1:7).

I. L-ove the Lord
"Love the Lord . . . with all thy heart . . . soul . . . mind" (Matt. 22:37).
- A. When you love God you give Him first place in your life. Pray daily. Read the Bible. Attend Church (the means of grace) faithfully.
- B. Prove your love for God by loving others and sharing Jesus Christ with the unsaved (1 John 3:14).

II. I-mitate the Lord
"Ye should follow his steps" (1 Peter 2:21).
- A. Many people imitate Satan; they walk in darkness, think evil thoughts, speak evil words, and commit evil deeds.
- B. Christians should seek to imitate the Lord in word, thought, deed, and action (John 13:15).

III. G-lorify the Lord
"Do all to the glory of God" (1 Cor. 10:31).
- A. Be Christlike in your home, work, and church. Your social life should not contradict Christian principles (1 Cor. 6:20).
- B. Witness to the lost and seek to lead them to saving knowledge of Jesus Christ.

IV. H-onor the Lord
"Honour the Lord with thy substance" (Prov. 3:9).
- A. The tithe, ten percent of one's earnings, should be brought to the house of God so that it can meet its financial obligations (Lev. 27:30).
- B. The institution of tithing was set up by God during Old Testament times. Jesus placed His sanction on it (Matt. 23:23).

V. T-rust the Lord

"Trust in the Lord with all thine heart" (Prov. 3:5).

A. By leaning on, relying on, and placing implicit faith in the Lord, we allow Him to glorify Himself through us.

B. God responds to our trust. He helps us in time of need. He works all things together for our good and His glory (Rom. 8:28).

47. How to Win Life's Race

"Let us run with patience the race that is set before us, looking unto Jesus the author and finisher of our faith" (Heb. 12:1-2).

I. Get Ready

"Be ye therefore ready also: for the Son of man cometh at an hour when ye think not" (Luke 12:40).

A. We prepare for His coming when we repent and forsake sin (2 Peter 3:9).

B. Repentance must be accompanied by faith (Acts 16:31).

C. The Christian must commit his life to Christ. This requires total dedication (Rom. 12:1).

II. Get Set

"Set your affections on things above, not on things on the earth" (Col. 3:2).

A. We become established in the faith by setting our love on spiritual things (Col. 2:7).

B. By praying, meditating on God's Word, and faithfully attending God's house, we become rooted and grounded in the faith.

C. Dedication and determination must be continued.

III. Go

"I will go in the strength of the Lord God" (Ps. 71:16).

A. We must go for God, not in our own strength but in the strength He gives.

B. We must go in prayer. The power and influence of prayer can reach around the world.

C. We must go in person. If we want to win life's race, we must call, invite, and witness for the Lord.

D. We must go until the race is finished. There is no stopping place this side of heaven (2 Tim. 4:7-8).

48. How to Win with Christ

"I press toward the mark for the prize of the high calling of God in Christ Jesus" (Phil. 3:14).

I. Live in Him

"If any man be in Christ, he is a new creature . . ." (2 Cor. 5:17).

A. "Be" in Christ—by repenting of sin and accepting Him as personal Savior.

B. "A new creature"—by doing those things that are pleasing to Him, we have a new life, new hope, new desires, and a new ambition.

II. Learn from Him

"[The Scriptures] were written for our learning, that we . . . might have hope" (Rom. 15:4).

A. The Word of God—the Bible—teaches us how we should live.

B. Christ teaches us—through His Word—His will for our lives. He leads, guides, and directs us. (Ps. 37:23).

III. Lean on Him

"Trust in the Lord . . . lean not upon thine own understanding" (Prov. 3:5).

A. When we trust in the Lord we need not worry about the future. As He took care of us yesterday, He takes care of us today, and He will take care of us tomorrow.

B. Rely on Him. By depending on the Lord, we become channels through which He can work. (Ps. 37:5).

IV. Listen to Him

"The sheep hear his voice: and he . . . leadeth them out" (John 10:3).

A. Christ speaks to us—sometimes through His Word, sometimes through providential means, and often through the Holy Spirit.

B. We must listen. He may speak loudly and clearly. Or, He may speak in a "still small voice," through a feeling, or a thought (John 10:4).

V. Labor with Him

"For we are labourers together with God" (1 Cor. 3:9).

A. Witness to others—work, pray, call, persuade others to accept Christ.

B. Workers together—the Lord goes with us. We are not alone. By faith, we believe He speaks through us; He gives us the right words at the right time and place.

VI. Look for Him

"Looking for the blessed hope, and the glorious appearance . . . of Jesus Christ" (Titus 2:13).

A. "That blessed hope"—the coming of Christ is the answer for Christians around the world.

B. Be prepared, for we know not the day or hour of His return. We only know He is coming (Matt. 24:44).

49. How to Wise Up to S-A-T-A-N

"Be sober, be vigilant; because your adversary the devil, as a roaring lion, walketh about, seeking whom he may devour" (1 Peter 5:8).

I. S-ubtle

"The serpent beguiled Eve through his subtilty" (2 Cor. 11:3).

A. Satan is sly; he attacks without notice. He masquerades as an angel of light (2 Cor. 11:14).

B. Therefore, we must be watchful and prayerful, resisting the devil and drawing nigh to God (James 4:7-8).

II. A-fflicter

"Satan . . . smote Job with sore boils . . ." (Job 2:7).

A. Satan afflicts God's people with trouble, sickness, worry, and torment.

B. God is greater, more powerful than Satan. He will deliver, help, heal, and strengthen those who trust Him (1 John 4:4).

III. T-empter

"He was there in the wilderness forty days tempted of Satan" (Mark 1:13).

A. Satan tried to get Christ to yield to the lust of the flesh, for power and fame.

B. Satan uses the same pattern today. He uses the lust of the flesh—illicit sex; the lust for power—the love of money; the lust for fame—the desire for popularity (1 Thess. 3:5).

IV. A-ccuser

"The accuser of our brethren is cast down . . ." (Rev. 12:10).

A. Satan accuses Christians of defeat, failure, hypocrisy, and evil.

B. We must declare, as Christ did, "Get thee behind me Satan!" and defeat him through faith (Eph. 6:16).

V. N-ational Deceiver

"Satan . . . shall go out to deceive the nations" (Rev. 20:7-8).

A. Satan is trying to delude, defraud, and defeat God's power, people, and purpose.

B. Our national defense is in God. His power, love, and grace are more than a match for Satan. We are conquerors through Him (Rom 8:37-39).

50. How to Avoid Quenching the Spirit

"Quench not the Spirit" (1 Thess. 5:19).

I. Don't Quibble
"Rooted and built up in him, and stablished in the faith" (Col. 2:7).
- A. Many Christians are not dependable. You never know where to find them. They are spiritually ineffective.
- B. They need to become established in the faith. We should know who we are, what we are, and where we are going (James 5:8).

II. Don't Quarrel
". . . forbearing one another in love; endeavouring to keep the unity of the Spirit in the bond of peace" (Eph. 4:2-3).
- A. Some people are disagreeable and complain about everything. They displease God by stirring up anger and strife.
- B. We must love one another. Through prayer and effort we can "keep the unity of the Spirit in the bond of peace" (See Ps. 133:1).

III. Don't Quail
"Wait on the Lord: be of good courage, and he shall strengthen thine heart" (Ps. 27:14).
- A. Many fail to make the spiritual progress they should. They falter when under trial, or they shrink at the prospect of witnessing for God.
- B. We must be courageous. We avoid quenching the Spirit when we go bravely forward to do, be, and say for God (Josh. 1:9).

IV. Don't Quit
". . . as workers together with him . . ." (2 Cor. 6:1).
- A. Some believers lack spiritual power. When adversity strikes, they throw up their hands and quit.
- B. The Holy Spirit gives inner strength. When we surrender all to Him, we are enabled to work, witness, and win through Him. "Ye are my witnesses" (Isa. 43:10).

51. How to Be a Successful Christian

". . . thou shalt make thy way prosperous, and then thou shalt have good success" (Josh. 1:8).

I. Right Concept
". . . whatsoever things are of good report . . . think on these things" (Phil. 4:8).
A. A right concept preceeds success in any endeavor.
B. "Possibility thinking" is necessary for the Christian. He must consider his difficulties, burdens, and problems as stepping stones and opportunities (Phil. 4:13).

II. Reliable Conduct
"In all things shewing thyself a pattern of good works" (Titus 2:7).
A. To be effective witnesses for God, we must set an example of good works. They are often more effective than good words.
B. To be good examples we must not only *do* good but we must *be* good. God looks on the heart.

III. Realistic Concern
". . . shew mercy and compassions every man to his brother" (Zech. 7:9).
A. Christ displayed compassion. He was concerned about the deepest needs of mankind.
B. We also need to be compassionate. We must help the needy, and pray for the sick and sinful.

IV. Ready Courage
"Be strong and of a good courage . . . for the Lord thy God is with thee . . ." (Josh. 1:9).
A. Courage is needed to work, warn, witness, and win. Christians need to be bold for God.
B. Courage comes through faith. God assures us of His help and presence as we work for Him.

V. Royal Conquest

". . . this is the victory that overcometh the world, even our faith" (1 John 5:4).

A. Victory is promised here and now to those who pray, work, and believe.

B. Futuristic victory is assured to the faithful. Jesus has promised to return and receive them unto Himself (John 14:1-3).

52. How to Be a Winner

"I can do all things through Christ which strengtheneth me" (Phil. 4:13).

I. Be Prayerful

"... in everything by prayer ... let your requests be made known unto God" (Phil. 4:6).

A. Those who do not pray do not win. They fail because they depend on their own strength.

B. God's power is released through prayer. God never fails. We win as we depend on Him (Matt. 21:22).

II. Be Positive

"... whatsoever things are of good report ... think on these things" (Phil. 4:8).

A. Those who have negative attitudes fail. They look for and expect the worst and, as a result, they receive it.

B. We must look for the good and expect the best. Faith pleases God and brings the victory (1 John 5:4).

III. Be Purposeful

"... the things which happened unto me have fallen out rather unto the furtherance of the gospel" (Phil. 1:12).

A. The apostle Paul was a winner. The purpose of his life was to further the gospel of Jesus Christ.

B. We need a purpose for living, too. We glorify God as we let Him speak through us (Rom. 14:7-8).

IV. Be Persuasive

"... he that winneth souls is wise" (Prov. 11:30).

A. Many fail in their soul-winning attempts. They are unconvincing because they lack concern and courage.

B. We should witness to the lost with persuasion, realizing that the value of a soul is beyond estimation (Matt. 18:11).

V. Be Persevering

"... I have suffered the loss of all things, and do count them but dung, that I may win Christ" (Phil. 3:8).

A. St. Paul suffered many things for Christ. He never gave up. He was a winner.

B. Troubles, trials, and testings come to everyone. We can win, too, if we "keep on keeping on" (See Rom. 12:12).

53. How to Be an Effective Christian

"He that saith he abideth in him ought himself also so to walk, even as he walked" (1 John 2:6).

I. Be Unselfish

".. . *be ye doers of the word, and not hearers only . . ." (James 1:22).*

A. Christ was never selfish. He lived His life for others, and He gave His life for others.

B. We too must be unselfish. We must give ourselves in total commitment to God, letting Him use us to help and bless others (James 2:15-16).

II. Be Understanding

".. . *shew mercy and compassions every man to his brother" (Zech. 7:9).*

A. Christ felt compassion for all people. He understood their suffering, sorrow, and sinfulness.

B. We also must be understanding. Effective Christians feel sympathy for those with infirmities, and for those who undergo testings and trials.

III. Be Useful

"For we are labourers together with God" (1 Cor. 3:9).

A. Christ not only understands, but helps the needy, lifts the fallen, and saves the sinful.

B. We also should help the less fortunate. We must witness in order to bring the lost to the acceptance of Christ's saving power (Rom. 12:11).

IV. Be Undaunted

".. . *he it is that doth go before thee . . . fear not, neither be dismayed" (Deut. 31:8).*

A. Christ was courageous. He faced His accusers fearlessly. Not even death could hold Him.

B. In the same way, we must serve the Lord with boldness. He is with us; He goes before us as we work and witness for Him (Deut. 31:6).

V. Be Uplifted

"And I, if I be lifted up from the earth, will draw all men unto me" (John 12:32).

A. Jesus Christ was lifted up. He came forth victorious over death and the grave.
B. We can be uplifted, too. We can be effective for Christ when He has set us free from the bondage of sin. "If the Son therefore shall make you free, ye shall be free indeed" (John 8:36).

54. How to Be Confident in God

"Beloved, if our heart condemn us not, then have we confidence toward God" (1 John 3:21).

I. Through Forgiveness

"If we confess our sins, he is faithful and just to forgive us our sins . . ." (1 John 1:9).

A. Unforgiven sin is accompanied by guilt. Those who lack God's forgiveness cannot be confident in Him.

B. Forgiveness is received by confession. When we repent and believe, we can be confident in God. Guilt disappears (Mark 11:25).

II. Through Freedom

". . . where the Spirit of the Lord is, there is liberty" (2 Cor. 3:17).

A. Many believers do not possess the fullness of the Spirit. They are not totally committed, and are limited by doubts and resentments.

B. The Holy Spirit brings freedom. His abiding Presence banishes bondage, frees us from Satanic entrapments, and increases confidence (Gal. 5:1).

III. Through Fervor

"Not slothful in business; fervent in spirit; serving the Lord" (Rom. 12:11).

A. Those with selfish motives are slothful about God's work. Their distorted purpose brings failure and defeat.

B. Christians should find delight in serving the Lord. As they fervently work, witness, and win for Him, their confidence grows.

IV. Through Faith

"Let us draw near with a true heart in full assurance of faith . . ." (Heb. 10:22).

A. Many displease God and disappoint themselves because of their lack of faith (Heb. 11:6).

B. Faith—confidence—is the means by which we open ourselves up to God. It is also the way to be victorious in Christ (1 John 5:4).

55. How to Be Faithful

"Be thou faithful unto death, and I will give thee a crown of life" (Rev. 2:10).

I. Be Dedicated

". . . present your bodies a living sacrifice, holy, acceptable unto God . . ." (Rom. 12:1).

A. Some devote their lives to projects, positions, or possessions. They pursue time, talents, and treasures.

B. We should be dedicated to God, seeking His will, way, and work. We should give Him first place in our lives (Ps. 37:5).

II. Be Disciplined

"Blessed is the man that endureth temptation" (James 1:12).

A. Undisciplined believers fail to accomplish what they should, or be the blessing for God that they should be.

B. Self-control and restraint must be practiced. We must set rules and limits for ourselves if we are to glorify God.

III. Be Determined

". . . be ye steadfast, unmovable . . . abounding in the work of the Lord . . ." (1 Cor. 15:58).

A. Some lack will power and determination. Like the seeds that fall on shallow soil, they cannot stand when testing comes.

B. Our determination is supplemented by the power of God. He is more than a match for Satan; we can conquer through Him (Phil. 4:13).

IV. Be Diligent

"For . . . your work and labour of love . . . we desire that every one of you do shew the same diligence . . ." (Heb. 6:10-11).

A. Many are slothful about worshiping and working for God. They are primarily interested in temporal pursuits.

B. The faithful are diligent for God. They encourage their fellow Christians, help the needy, and witness to the lost.

V. Be Dependable

". . . make you perfect, stablish, strengthen, settle you" (1 Peter 5:10).

A. Some habitually fail in their duties to God and man. They are undependable and will be judged for their unfaithfulness.
B. Disappointment and discouragement come to all. Those who are steadfast will be found worthy to receive the crown of life (Rev. 2:10).

56. How to Be H-A-P-P-Y

"Happy is he that hath the God of Jacob for his help, whose hope is in the Lord his God" (Ps. 146:5).

I. H-elpful
". . . do good . . . be rich in good works, ready to distribute . . . " (1 Tim. 6:18).
A. Selfish people are discontented. They work primarily for sinful pleasures and material possessions, which are not satisfying.
B. Helpful people are happy people. As they assist the poor, visit the sick, and witness to the lost, they experience a feeling of accomplishment.

II. A-dventurous
"I can do all things through Christ which strengtheneth me" (Phil. 4:13).
A. Many people lack faith and courage. They are in bondage to their feelings of inadequacy.
B. Happy Christians reach out to be, see, go, and do. Their adventurous faith is a blessing to others.

III. P-ositive
". . . whatsoever things are of good report; . . . if there be any praise, think on these things" (Phil. 4:8).
A. People with negative attitudes are spiritually stunted and unhappy. Their outreach is destined to failure.
B. Being positive brings joy and success. We should practice looking for the good and encouraging others.

IV. P-urposeful
". . . follow after righteousness, godliness, faith, love, patience, meekness" (1 Tim. 6:11).
A. Life must be directed. Without purpose it becomes dwarfed, defeated, and is soon dissipated.
B. Christ gives meaning to life. Living for Him brings faith, love, hope, and the promise of eternal life.

V. Y-ielded
". . . present your bodies a living sacrifice, holy, acceptable unto God, which is your reasonable service" (Rom. 12:1).

A. Those who do not surrender their will to God's will are dissatisfied. Their usefulness is limited.
B. Totally committed people are happy people. With access to the infinite power of God, their potential accomplishments are unlimited.

57. How to Be U

"If a man therefore purge himself . [...] master's use . . ." (2 Tim. 2:21).

VI. Let Him go th [...] the Lo [...] (Josh. 1:9 [...] A. God [...] B. H [...] VII. [...]

I. Let Him think through you
". . . I will put my laws into th
will I write them" (Heb. 10:16)
A. God can put thoughts and ide
used to bless others and glor
B. God needs your cooperatio
thinking; fill your mind with

II. Let Him see through your ey
"But mine eyes are unto thee, O God the Lord" (Ps. 141:8).
A. The devil attempts to distract and divert our attention—
through the lust of the flesh, the love of money, and the
lure of sinful pleasure.
B. The Lord wants to see through our eyes. He wants us to
see the hurts and sufferings of others.

III. Let Him hear through your ears
"And it was revealed in mine ears by the Lord . . ." (Isa.
22:14).
A. Much of television communicates non-Christian values.
Foul language, illicit sex, and violence are common. These
are not the kinds of things a Christian should use his ears
for.
B. The Lord wants you to use your ears to hear the cries of
the lost, the frustrated, the needy.

IV. Let Him speak through your voice
"For it is not ye that speak, but the Spirit of your Father which
speaketh in you" (Matt. 10:20).
A. God speaks His words through teachers and ministers to
meet the needs of His people.
B. Christians should recognize that God speaks through
them as they witness to others about Jesus Christ.

V. Let Him work through your hands
". . . the Father that dwelleth in me . . . doeth the works"
(John 14:10).
A. Willing workers are needed in the Master's vineyard.
B. When you are willing to use your hands to assist in the
maintenance of God's property, He will reward you.

...rough your feet

...d ... is with thee whithersoever thou goest"

...).

...seeks the lost, the hopeless, and the helpless.

...e needs your feet to go for Him. Trust Him for direction.

...et Him love through your heart

"*. . . let us love one another"* (1 John 4:7).

A. Love is a built-in psychological need. Every person needs to love and to be loved.

B. Let God's love reach out through you to meet that need in the world.

58. How to Be Your Best Self

". . . greater is he that is in you, than he that is in the world" (1 John 4:4).

I. Be Genuine

". . . speaking the truth in love" (Eph. 4:15).

A. Many practice hypocrisies. They are insincere. Their lives are shams.

B. We must be honest with God, ourselves, and others. Always be "for real" (See 1 Thess. 5:21-22).

II. Be Gracious

". . . be ye kind one to another . . ." (Eph. 4:32).

A. Some are ungracious to the less fortunate. God is not pleased with this.

B. Thoughtfulness, kindness, courtesy, and understanding to all people bring God's approval and lift one to one's best self (Gal. 5:22-23).

III. Be Generous

"Give, and it shall be given unto you" (Luke 6:38).

A. The Lord gave Himself for us. He died on the cross for our sins. He gave His all.

B. The Lord loves the cheerful giver. We should give liberally of our abilities and our possessions (Mal. 3:10-11).

IV. Be Gallant

"In whom we have boldness and access with confidence by the faith of him" (Eph. 3:12).

A. Courage is needed for one to be at one's best. It should be accompanied by courtesy and kindness.

B. Christians need boldness to present the gospel to others in the same measure as they have received it (Prov. 28:1).

V. Be Grateful

"In every thing give thanks" (1 Thess. 5:18).

A. When we show appreciation to others, they receive a blessing, and our self-esteem is lifted.

B. We should be thankful to God for His sacrifice and salvation. The more grateful we are to Him, the greater He is to us (Ps. 100:4).

59. How to Cope with Trying Circumstances

"And we know that all things work together for good to them that love God, to them who are the called according to his purpose" (Rom. 8:28).

I. The Weather
"Stand still, and consider the wondrous works of God" (Job 37:14).
A. Many go to work under the most adverse weather conditions, but they neglect the church under the same circumstances.
B. We must give God first place. We will be a blessing and receive a reward if we reject Satan's "fair weather" excuses (Matt. 6:33).

II. The Wallet
"Give, and it shall be given unto you" (Luke 6:38).
A. Some are generous toward themselves and other people, but tight-fisted with God, using His tithe for selfish pursuits.
B. We must share with God first. He will multiply the remainder and supply our needs (Phil. 4:19).

III. The Worries
"Take . . . no (anxious) thought for the morrow" (Matt. 6:34).
A. Troubles and trials come to all. But they serve as stumbling blocks to many believers, causing them to flounder and fall.
B. However, difficulties and distresses may be used as stepping stones. We should utilize our trying circumstances. With our faith and God's help we can reach the highest and best (Phil. 4:13).

IV. The Waiting
". . . they that wait upon the Lord shall renew their strength" (Isa. 40:31).
A. Many Christians lack patience. Waiting can be most difficult, but it also can be most rewarding.
B. Patience teaches us faith and faith pleases God. Faith brings forgiveness, strength, miracles, and victories (1 John 5:4).

60. How to Define S-A-V-I-O-U-R

"And we have seen and do testify that the Father sent the Son to be the Saviour of the world" (1 John 4:14).

I. S-acrifice

". . . he . . . put away sin by the sacrifice of himself" (Heb. 9:26).

A. Some have died for their country, for friends or loved ones, but their deaths could not atone for sin.

B. Christ's sacrifice on the cross was supreme. He died once and for all, for the sins of the world.

II. A-dvocate

". . . we have an advocate with the Father, Jesus Christ the righteous" (1 John 2:1).

A. An advocate is: "A person who pleads in another's behalf; an intercessor."

B. Christ is the Christian's advocate. If any believer sins, he can have forgiveness through Him.

III. V-ictor

"He will swallow up death in victory" (Isa. 25:8).

A. Christ was victorious in temptation, trial, and testing. Death, hell, and the grave could not defeat Him.

B. We, also, can conquer through Christ (1 Cor. 15:57).

IV. I-deal

". . . Christ also suffered for us, leaving us an example, that ye should follow his steps" (1 Peter 2:21).

A. When faced with trying circumstances, we should ask ourselves, "What would Jesus do?"

B. When we follow Christ's example we can be confident that we are making the right decisions.

V. O-vercomer

". . . be of good cheer; I have overcome the world" (John 16:33).

A. Christ was calm and peaceful when others were distraught and frustrated. He overcame the world.

B. Christ enables us to be overcomers, too. Daily prayer, trust, and obedience assure us of victory.

VI. U-niversal

". . . the Father sent the Son to be the Saviour of the world"
(1 John 4:14).

A. All who repent and believe on Jesus Christ are redeemed.

B. Christ has no prejudices. He came to save those of every race, nationality, social status (John 3:16).

VII. R-ewarder

". . . he is a rewarder of them that diligently seek him" (Heb. 11:6).

A. Answered prayer awaits those who serve God diligently.

B. Eternal life awaits those who believe on Jesus Christ.

61. How to Describe Our Heavenly Home

". . . Eye hath not seen, nor ear heard, neither have entered into the heart of man, the things which God hath prepared for them that love him" (1 Cor. 2:9).

I. A Purchased Home
". . . These . . . have washed their robes . . . in the blood of the Lamb" (Rev. 7:14).
A. Our earthly homes are usually obtained by work and worry, payments and penalties, sacrifice and struggle.
B. Our heavenly home was purchased by the blood of Christ. It is reserved for those who have been redeemed. Heaven is a holy place for a holy people (Rev. 21:27).

II. A Prepared Home
"I go to prepare a place for you" (John 14:2).
A. Earthly homes are sometimes built with shoddy material and workmanship. They are temporal and prone to deteriorate.
B. The Lord spoke the planets, the stars, and all of creation into existence. His work is always magnificent. He is preparing our heavenly home, which is eternal.

III. A Peaceful Home
". . . there shall be no more death . . . sorrow . . . crying . . . pain: for the former things are passed away" (Rev. 21:4).
A. Many homes are without Christ. Some are torn with heartache and strife, some with separation and divorce.
B. The presence of the Lord will permeate our heavenly home. Peace, harmony, and love will abound.

IV. A Protected Home
". . . lay up . . . treasures in heaven . . . where thieves do not break through and steal" (Matt. 6:20).
A. Earthly homes are subject to earthquakes, tornadoes, thefts, fire, and decay. They are unprotected.
B. Our heavenly home will be protected from the elements; there will be no riots, destruction, or decay. God will dwell among us (Rev. 21:3).

V. A Pleasurable Home

"At thy right hand there are pleasures for evermore" (Ps. 16:11).

A. Many homes are drab, unhappy abodes. They contain little joy because they do not have Christ within.

B. In our heavenly home there will be no more sin, sorrow, sickness, sadness—ever. It will be filled with the joy of the Lord. God Himself will be there (Rev. 22:3-5).

62. How to Describe the Blood-bought

"For ye are bought with a price: therefore glorify God in your body, and in your spirit, which are God's" (1 Cor. 6:20).

I. Purchased
"Take heed . . . to feed the church of God, which he hath purchased with his own blood" (Acts 20:28).
A. Man sinned. He fell from grace, losing his first estate. His disobedience and sin separated him from God.
B. Jesus Christ bled and died on the cross for all men. He thereby purchased us, bringing us back into fellowship with God (1 Thess. 5:9-10).

II. Pardoned
". . . being now justified by his blood, we shall be saved . . . through him" (Rom. 5:9).
A. Those who reject God cannot receive His forgiveness. Pardon is possible for all—the "whosoever wills" (See John 3:16).
B. Forgiveness awaits those who repent of their sins and believe on the Lord Jesus Christ (Eph. 1:7).

III. Purified
". . . the blood of Jesus Christ his Son cleanseth us from all sin" (1 John 1:7).
A. Some fail to surrender all to God. They persist in having their own will, and fall short of being "cleansed from all sin."
B. God wants first place in our life. We are sanctified through Christ's blood when we totally commit ourselves to Him (1 Thess. 4:3).

IV. Preserved
". . . I pray God your whole spirit and soul and body be preserved blameless . . ." (1 Thess. 5:23).
A. Many fail to accept Christ because they feel they are unable to live the Christian life. And that is true—they cannot live the Christian life in their own power.
B. Christ helps and keeps us. When we are totally committed to Him, we are preserved (2 Tim. 1:12).

V. Productive

". . . I have chosen you . . . that ye should go and bring forth fruit . . ." (John 15:16).

A. Some want only to receive benefits from God. They fail in their Christian experience because they do not work for God by giving out to others.

B. We live productively when we serve in God's house, help the needy, and witness to the unsaved (Luke 14:23).

63. How to Describe the Sanctified

"Wherefore Jesus also, that he might sanctify the people with his own blood, suffered without the gate" (Heb. 13:12).

I. They Are Purified
". . . purifying their hearts by faith" (Acts 15:9).
A. The fall of mankind brought sin and pollution to all. Repentance and faith bring forgiveness of sins.
B. Total commitment in faith brings the cleansing and infilling of God's love (1 John 1:9).

II. They Are Satisfied
". . . he satisfieth the longing soul . . ." (Ps. 107:9).
A. Many are seeking something to satisfy the emptiness and longing in their lives.
B. Jesus Christ offers peace and contentment to those who place their faith and confidence in Him (Phil. 4:7).

III. They Are Fortified
". . . I give you power . . . over all the power of the enemy" (Luke 10:19).
A. God is the source of all power. He is omnipotent.
B. The Holy Spirit gives strength, courage, protection, and direction to those who are devoted to Him.

IV. They Are Occupied
"And he called his ten servants . . . and said unto them, Occupy till I come" (Luke 19:13).
A. Christians should be occupied with prayer, Bible reading, church attendance, church support, and helping the needy.
B. Christians need to be occupied in witnessing to the lost, and in seeking to bring them to a saving knowledge of Jesus Christ (2 Cor. 6:1).

V. They Will Be Glorified
". . . the dead shall be raised incorruptible, and we shall be changed" (1 Cor. 15:52).
A. Christians are subjected to trouble, trial, suffering, sorrow, deterioration, and death here on earth.
B. When Christ appears, we shall be changed to His likeness, raised incorruptible, and shall reign with Him forever (Col. 3:4).

64. How to Discern the Deeds of the Devil

"For this purpose the Son of God was manifested, that he might destroy the works of the devil" (1 John 3:8).

I. The Devil Distracts
"Lest Satan should get an advantage of us: for we are not ignorant of his devices" (2 Cor. 2:11).
A. Satan is transformed into an angel of light. He attracts, distracts, and attacks (2 Cor. 11:14).
B. We must resist the devil and draw nearer to God by watching and praying (James 4:7-8).

II. The Devil Deceives
". . . Satan . . . shall go out to deceive the nations . . ." (Rev. 20:7-8).
A. Satan tries to frustrate God's people. His deception may cause the wrong to seem right and the right to seem wrong.
B. Through prayer, faith, and God's Word we are enabled to discern the difference. We are conquerors through Him (Rom. 8:37-39).

III. The Devil Disgraces
". . . the serpent beguiled Eve through his subtilty . . ." (2 Cor. 11:3).
A. Satan uses temptation to bring many to disgrace. He tempts through illicit sex, the love of money, and the desire for popularity (1 Thess. 3:5).
B. We can defeat Satan through faith (Eph. 6:16). Let us declare as Christ did, "Get thee behind me, Satan."

IV. The Devil Depresses
". . . Satan . . . smote Job with sore boils . . ." (Job 2:7).
A. Satan discourages God's people. He afflicts them with testing, trial, trouble, and torment.
B. God will help and heal, strengthen and sustain those who trust Him. He is greater than Satan (1 John 4:4).

V. The Devil Destroys

"For the wages of sin is death; but the gift of God is eternal life . . ." (Rom. 6:23).

A. Satan is in the sin business. His ultimate desire is to defeat God and destroy His people (1 Peter 5:8).

B. Since God is more than a match for Satan, Satan is doomed for defeat. He shall be cast down and destroyed (Rev. 12:10).

65. How to Do the Impossible

"... if ye have faith ... nothing shall be impossible unto you" (Matt. 17:20).

I. Ponder the Purpose of Faith
"That we might receive the promise of the Spirit through faith" (Gal. 3:14).
A. Faith is the means by which we receive God. When we ask in faith, He comes into our heart and life.
B. We also receive from God through faith. Love, joy, peace, hope, help, and even miracles come through prayer accompanied by faith.

II. Prove the Promises of Faith
"He staggered not at the promise of God through unbelief; but was strong in faith ..." (Rom. 4:20).
A. Test the promises of faith. They cannot fail because God cannot fail.
B. Try the promises of faith by using them in times of trial, adversity, and need. Our faith works as we work our faith (James 2:17-18).

III. Pursue the Possibilities of Faith
"... all things are possible to him that believeth" (Mark 9:23).
A. The potential of faith is beyond comprehension. "All things are possible." God is limited only by our failure to believe.
B. Persistence and patience are often required before we see God work. We must keep on believing while waiting for God to answer in His own time and way.

IV. Pray the Prayer of Faith
"If ye shall ask anything in my name, I will do it" (John 14:14).
A. Some people pray to express opinions. Some pray to impress other people. These are ineffective and faithless prayers.
B. Petitions made to God which are subject to His will and accompanied by faith bring results (Matt. 21:22).

V. Proclaim the Power of Faith

". . . ye shall say unto this mountain, Remove hence . . . and it shall remove" (Matt. 17:20).

A. Man has made progress in the development of power—horse power, steam power, water power, and atomic power.

B. But man cannot match the power of God. God's power far exceeds man's feeble attempts at development. God is omnipotent. He has given us access to His great power by faith (Rom. 1:16).

66. How to Do the Will of God

". . . the world passeth away . . . but he that doeth the will of God abideth for ever" (1 John 2:17).

I. Be Committed to God
"Commit thy way unto the Lord" (Ps. 37:5).
A. The Christian should surrender to God's will every day. Paul said, "I die daily."
B. The tasks ahead may seem too great, or they may seem too unimportant. Being yielded to God's will brings peace and victory in either case.

II. Be Contented with God
". . . godliness with contentment is great gain" (1 Tim. 6:6).
A. Circumstances may be adverse or favorable, but if we know we are in God's will, we can be satisfied.
B. We may be content even in the midst of trials if we realize God is working in our lives (Rom. 8:28).

III. Be Confident in God
". . . this is the confidence that we have in him . . . he heareth us" (1 John 5:14).
A. Our faith increases when it is challenged and put through the fire.
B. Confidence assures us of answered prayer (1 John 5:15). Confidence in God brings His favor, for faith pleases Him (Heb. 11:6).

IV. Be Constrained by God
"For the love of Christ constraineth us" (2 Cor. 5:14).
A. To be constrained means to be compelled.
B. Because of the force of His great love, Christians should feel compelled to share the gospel with others. Believers should not be able to keep Christ to themselves.

V. Be Courageous for God
". . . Be thou strong and very courageous" (Josh. 1:7).
A. We need boldness in witnessing if we are to "compel them to come in."
B. Courage is needed for the tasks of life. We need to assert with Paul, "I can do all things through Christ which strengtheneth me" (Phil. 4:13).

67. How to Experience God's Power

"For I am not ashamed of the gospel of Christ: for it is the power of God unto salvation to every one that believeth . . ." (Rom. 1:16).

I. Saving Power

"For whosoever shall call upon the name of the Lord shall be saved" (Rom. 10:13).

A. No amount of money, education, social standing, or scientific achievement can bring forgiveness of sins.

B. Only the power of God, through the gospel of Jesus Christ, can bring forgiveness. Eternal life is given to those who repent and believe.

II. Sanctifying Power

"Sanctify them through thy truth: thy word is truth" (John 17:17).

A. Through consecration and faith, Christians receive the cleansing and infilling of the Holy Spirit.

B. God gives His power to work, witness, and win others to Christ to those who are completely committed to Him (1 Thess. 5:23).

III. Satisfying Power

". . . the peace of God . . . shall keep your hearts and minds through Christ Jesus" (Phil. 4:7).

A. Ours is an age of distraction and discontentment. There are troubles and trials, suffering and sorrows all around us.

B. The power of God brings satisfaction. The Christian has peace and joy when he nurtures the right kind of thoughts (Phil. 4:8).

IV. Sustaining Power

"Who are kept by the power of God through faith" (1 Peter 1:5).

A. Some people want to be Christians, but they try to live the Christian life through their own power. This is impossible to do.

B. The sustaining power of God, through faith, keeps what we commit to Him—ourselves, our lives, our future (2 Tim. 1:12).

V. Stabilizing Power
"*. . . make you perfect, stablish, strengthen, settle you*" *(1 Peter 5:10).*

A. Many Christians fail to be a blessing because they are immature, unstable, and undependable.

B. Maturity, strength, and dependability are God's gifts to those who grow in grace and love. These gifts are attained through prayer, faith, patience, and obedience.

68. How to Explain the C-R-O-S-S

Scripture Reading: Matthew 16:24-26

". . . if any man will come after me, let him deny himself, and take up his cross, and follow me" (Matt. 16:24).

I. C-rucifixion
A. Consider Christ's death—He was innocent in life and death; He did not resist death, even though His was a humiliating death (1 Peter 2:21-24).
B. His death was effective (1 Peter 2:24).
   1. He died—in our stead—that we might live.
   2. He died because He loved us.

II. R-esurrection
A. Christ's death would have meant nothing without His resurrection.
B. The angel conveyed Christ's message (Matt. 28:6-7).
   1. The proclamation: "He is risen, as he said."
   2. The power: "He is risen from the dead."
   3. The presence: "He goeth before you . . . ye shall see him."

III. O-bedience
A. God and man meet at the center of the cross.
B. All that Christ has done and can do is at stake. Men can reject or accept the sacrifice.
   1. Christ's obedience—Phil. 2:8; Heb. 5:7-8.
   2. Our obedience—Acts 5:29.
   3. We may obey or disobey, whichever we choose—John 3:16.

IV. S-alvation
A. The cross means forgiveness for our sins (1 Peter 3:18; 1 John 2:2).
B. The cross means cleansing for our sanctification (Heb. 13:12; Rom. 6:6).
   1. Brings purity of heart and soul.
   2. Brings power for service.

V. S-acrifice
A. Christ's sacrifice was for our forgiveness and cleansing (Heb. 10:12-14).
B. We may be called to sacrifice our time, talent, or our treasures (Matt. 16:24-26).

69. How to Face the Future

"And the Lord, he it is that doth go before thee; he will be with thee, he will not fail thee, neither forsake thee: fear not, neither be dismayed" (Deut. 31:8).

I. With Confidence
"Being confident . . . that he which hath begun a good work in you will perform it until the day of Jesus Christ" (Phil. 1:6).
- A. Today's world is filled with turmoil and trouble. Many face the future with frustration and doubt.
- B. The believer can place his confidence in God and depend on Him. God is the One who never fails (Ps. 37:3).

II. With Commitment
"Commit thy way unto the Lord; trust also in him; and he shall bring it to pass" (Ps. 37:5).
- A. Many try to cope with life's challenges in their own strength and fail. Human power is finite.
- B. We must surrender our wills to God and be totally yielded to His will. We can depend on His infinite wisdom. He gives His power to those who are totally committed to Him (Rom. 12:1).

III. With Cheerfulness
"Delight thyself also in the Lord; and he shall give thee the desires of thine heart" (Ps. 37:4).
- A. Many Christians think negatively. They dwell on the gloomy side of life.
- B. We must think positively, looking for the good around us. We will be able to win others to Christ as we exemplify His love and joy (Phil. 4:4).

IV. With Courage
". . . with all boldness . . . Christ shall be magnified in my body . . ." (Phil. 1:20).
- A. The apostle Paul faced life courageously. He was able to cope with adversity through the power of Christ.
- B. We too must face the future with courage. Christ will go with us and before us as we work and witness for Him (Isa. 41:10).

70. How to "Get with it" for God

"Make you perfect in every good work to do his will, working in you that which is wellpleasing in his sight . . ." (Heb. 13:21).

I. Minimize Your Fears
". . . he saith unto them, It is I; be not afraid" (John 6:20)
A. Our world is dangerous. Violence and crime fill our streets, making them unsafe by day or night.
B. Christ is our Safety. He watches over, protects, and keeps those who commit their lives to Him (Mark 6:50).

II. Maximize Your Faith
". . . The just shall live by faith" (Rom. 1:17).
A. Many Christians lack faith. They disappoint themselves, discourage others, and defeat God's purposes.
B. Prayer, effort, and a positive attitude increase faith. Faith produces miracles, brings impossibilities to pass, and glorifies God (Mark 9:23).

III. Magnify Your Fervor
". . . fervent in spirit; serving the Lord" (Rom. 12:11).
A. Some Christians are uninterested and unconcerned about the needs of others. Because they are indifferent, they are ineffective.
B. We must be fervent in service for God. Prayer and ardent zeal bring results when presenting Christ to the lost (James 5:16).

IV. Manifest Your Freedom
"If the Son therefore shall make you free, ye shall be free indeed" (John 8:36).
A. Many are bound by doubts and resentments. They are unable to be the blessings they should be.
B. We must be aware of our God-given freedom. Christ can set us free from selfishness, resentment, hatred, and strife (Gal. 5:1).

V. Mobilize Your Forces

"The harvest truly is plenteous, but the labourers are few"
(Matt. 9:37).

A. Many Christians sit with folded hands. They fail to work in God's harvest field.

B. We must be about the Master's business. The field is ripe unto harvest. It is high time to witness, and win the lost to Christ (1 Cor. 3:9).

71. How to Handle Adversity

". . . after that ye have suffered a while, make you perfect, stablish, strengthen, settle you" (1 Peter 5:10).

I. Prayer
"The effectual fervent prayer of a righteous man availeth much" (James 5:16).
- A. Many people do not even pray when adversity strikes. They depend solely on human effort, and of course, they fail (Luke 18:1).
- B. Prayer changes things and people. Through prayer, we receive God's comfort and help in time of trouble (1 Thess. 5:17).

II. Promises
"Whereby are given unto us exceeding great and precious promises" (2 Peter 1:4).
- A. Some believers are defeated in times of difficulty because they do not appropriate God's promises to their needs.
- B. God's promises are powerful; they never fail. They can meet the deepest needs of those who believe them (1 Peter 5:7).

III. Patience
"But let patience have her perfect work, that ye may be perfect and entire, wanting nothing" (James 1:4).
- A. It is difficult to be patient in time of adversity. We become fretful and frustrated as the hardship continues.
- B. God has a purpose in what He allows for us. We should look for the good in each trial, and should wait patiently for His will to be worked out in our lives. (Rom. 8:28).

IV. Perseverance
". . . forgetting those things which are behind, and reaching forth . . . I press toward the mark . . ." (Phil. 3:13-14).
- A. Many give up when trouble strikes. They blame God or other people.
- B. We must be persistent, and keep working to improve difficult situations. We must have faith that God will see us through (Heb. 10:23).

V. Praise

"In every thing give thanks: for this is the will of God in Christ Jesus concerning you" (1 Thess. 5:18).

A. This command is sometimes difficult to obey. How can one praise God in the midst of adversity?

B. Praise the Lord, anyhow! He loves you. He died for you. When we praise, we look for the good and not the bad. Praise brings the victory (Ps. 113:2-3).

72. How to Explain God's G-R-A-C-E

Scripture Reading: Eph. 2:1-10.

"For by grace are ye saved through faith; and that not of yourselves: it is the gift of God" (Eph. 2:8).

I. G-oodness of God
". . . God . . . rich in mercy, for his great love wherewith he loved us" (Eph. 2:4).

A. Grace means "favor, kindness, mercy, forgiveness."

B. God's goodness is bestowed on His children each day. We should recognize His blessings—we should count them, name them, and be thankful for them (Heb. 13:15).

II. R-edemption by God
". . . God . . . hath quickened us together with Christ, (by grace ye are saved;)" (Eph. 2:5).

A. Man was made holy by God. Then he became degenerated by Satan and sin. Now he may be regenerated by Jesus Christ (Heb. 9:12).

B. Man must repent and receive Christ's redemption by believing in His work on the cross (Gal. 2:20).

III. A-ssistance from God
"That . . . he might shew the exceeding riches of his grace in his kindness toward us . . ." (Eph. 2:7).

A. To assist means to help. God can do what we cannot do. He helps in time of need (Heb. 4:16).

B. God has promised to supply all our needs, and we can rest assured that He keeps His word (Phil. 4:19).

IV. C-reated for God
". . . we are his workmanship, created in Christ Jesus unto good works . . ." (Eph. 2:10).

A. "Good works" include witnessing to others, lending a helping hand to the needy, worshiping faithfully, prayer, and Bible reading.

B. God works through surrendered Christians. Let Him work through you, doing those things that are pleasing in His sight (1 John 3:22).

V. E-ternity with God

"That in the ages to come he might shew the . . . riches of his grace . . ." (Eph. 2:7).

A. God's grace is sufficient to sustain us in this life.

B. God's grace provides an eternity with Himself for those who serve Him. Jesus has gone to prepare a place for those who have accepted His grace (John 14:2-3).

73. How to Be Liberated

"If the Son . . . shall make you free, ye shall be free indeed" (John 8:36).

I. Discover Christ

"Stand fast . . . in the liberty wherewith Christ hath made us free" (Gal. 5:1).

A. Christ sets us free from sin. Through repentance and faith we are forgiven, cleansed, and made spiritually whole.

B. Christ sets us free from sexual sins—adultery, fornication, and perversions. God will judge and punish those who commit such deeds (Gal. 5:19-21).

II. Develop Confidence

". . . this is the confidence that we have in him . . . he heareth us" (John 5:14).

A. Having placed our confidence in Christ, we are liberated from the fear of death and the judgment.

B. The more we trust in Christ and His promises the stronger our confidence becomes.

III. Disperse Compassion

". . . having compassion one of another . . ." (1 Peter 3:8).

A. Christ was filled with compassion and understanding. He wants us to care for others, too.

B. A concern for others brings freedom from resentment and self-centeredness.

IV. Distribute Cheerfulness

"A merry heart maketh a cheerful countenance" (Prov. 15:13).

A. Cheerfulness liberates one from gloom, sadness, and discouragement. God is pleased when we rejoice in Him.

B. Cheerfulness increases our effectiveness for God. It is evidence of the joy Christ gives.

V. Display Courage

". . . be thou strong and very courageous . . ." (Josh. 1:7).

A. Courage liberates one from cowardliness. A courageous Christian bravely takes his stand and moves ahead for God.

B. A courageous Christian accepts the challenge to live and lift, to grow and go, to witness and win for the Lord.

74. How to Be an Overcomer

"To him that overcometh will I grant to sit with me in my throne, even as I also overcame . . ." (Rev. 3:21).

I. Prevail in Prayer
"The effectual fervent prayer of a righteous man availeth much" (James 5:16).
A. All our victories begin with prayer. Every failure and sin can be forgiven by asking God's pardon.
B. All our trials and troubles may be taken to God and left with Him. We overcome testings through prayer (1 Thess. 5:17).

II. Pursue the Promises
"Whereby are given us exceeding great and precious promises" (2 Peter 1:4).
A. God's promises are given for our salvation. "That by these ye might be partakers of the divine nature . . ." (2 Peter 1:4).
B. The promises are given for our learning. Through them we can find God's will, instruction, and guidance.

III. Persist in Patience
"But let patience have her perfect work . . ." (James 1:4).
A. Most of us lack patience. God sometimes allows troubles and trials to come so our patience can increase.
B. We learn patience by waiting on the Lord. It takes time for an oak to grow or for an artist to paint a rose (Heb. 10:36).

IV. Proclaim His Praise
"Let everything that hath breath praise the Lord" (Ps. 150:6).
A. God desires our praise—for everything (1 Thess. 5:18).
B. God hears our praise. It often moves His arm when nothing else can, and enables us to overcome.

V. Promote His Purpose
". . . the eternal purpose which he purposed in Christ . . ." (Eph. 3:11).
A. We promote God's purpose when we witness to the lost and seek to bring them to a saving knowledge of Jesus Christ (2 Peter 3:9).
B. We promote God's purpose when we faithfully serve Him with our time, talent, and treasure. We overcome by working for God.